GETTING THERE

To: Marliesse
Find what you love,
and do it!

[signature] 1/29/11

GETTING THERE

VOLUME 2

(IT'S NOT ABOUT THE RESUMÉ)

Luis A. Martínez

HTTP://GettingThereCoach.com

To order additional copies of this book, contact:
Xlibris Corporation
1-888-795-4274
www.Xlibris.com
Orders@Xlibris.com
59166

CONTENTS

Questions You Hope They Don't Ask; Illegal Questions That Employers Should Never Ask; Some Exceptions; Two: The T-Chart Their Needs and Your Contributions; Three: The Questions That You Must Ask; Preparing for the Second Interview; Tips and Tactics for Interviewing; Do's and Don'ts for Interviewing; Handling Rejection; Your Sunshine Folder; How to Handle Exploratory Interviews; The Purpose of This Interview Is—To Get the Next Interview!; What Are They Really Buying? Your Attributes!; It's Really about Turning Your Passion into Opportunity; A Good Interviewer Is Hard to Find; How to Handle the Telephone Interview; Immediately After the Interview; Chapter Summary; Homework

What if They Ask My Salary?; Negotiating for the Optimal Salary; Salary Structures; What if You Can't Come to Terms?; Are You a Good Advocate for Self?; Chapter Summary

Your 100-Day Plan, Chapter Summary

Unemployed?; Don't Look at Rejection; The Dangers of the Comfort Zone; Beleaguered and Becalmed; Comfort Zone Disposition = Disastrous Consequences; A Mole in His Hole; On the Importance of Meeting People; The Two-Million-Dollar Tip; Ask for Help; On Collaboration; On Exchanging Business Cards; For Networking Meetings; For Exploratory Interviews; What about Working with Headhunters?; Using Groups to Advance Your Search; Powerful SIGs; Steps to Lifelong Networking; On Networking—an Expert's Viewpoint; Visualizing the Ideal New Job; Visualizing My Book at Wegmans; Visualizing in Great Detail; Preemptive Buyer's Remorse; Performance Management; Top 7 Characteristics of the Best; Supersize Your Dream; Summary; Homework

It is not because things are difficult that we do not dare;
it is because we do not dare that they are difficult.
—Lucius Annaeus Seneca

Dedicated to my father

José Luis Martínez

La Habana, Cuba
1921-2008

ACKNOWLEDGMENTS

I have many, many people to thank for this book. As of this second edition, I have worked with several hundred clients. *Client* is the word that I use to describe the business relationship that I maintain with my readers as we work using this book. But *client* is not the right word to describe what all of you mean to me. The truth is that I have learned more from you in the aggregate, my client friends, than can be learned from using this career search process. You shared deep and personal aspects of your life with me. You trusted in me. And for that—I am ever so grateful.

And other readers are grateful, too, because the knowledge, tactics, information—wisdom—that emanates from each client encounter is then included in this book, which is later used to help the next person. As I meet with people and help them, I think of design and implement new tools and techniques that enable and assist others.

The list of wonderful people who have helped me includes the following: my board of advisors (John Bernacki, Robert Colangelo, Sean Flaherty, Roger O'Brien, and Marcia Olson) for their wisdom and encouragement; Julio Ahumada for being an awesome friend; Lisbeth Arellano for her support of my office in Miami; Patty Brown, Dena Germano, and Jean Ticen for sharing *The Secret*; the Canaltown Coffee Roasters gang (Juan, Joe, Jim, Matt, Mario, and owner Peter) for keeping me honest; Jane Fairchild, for editing and contributions to networking and cold/warm calling; our networking group of executives, the executive network (GTEN) for their advocacy; Kelly L. Hayden for her encouraging support; Christine "Stina" Kennedy for book jacket design; Tony Karakashian for taking a chance and adding me to the speakers roster for TEDx Rochester; Robert Kostin and Kelly Cheatle for their patience with me as they invigorated and improved my Web sites; Cheri Magin for her contribution to the section "The First 100 Days"; Karen Marley for editing my blog posts—with a smile; Hannah Morgan for her subject matter expertise and advice; Karen Mungenast for her advocacy and encouragement; Clay Osborne for opening my eyes to my *Blue Ocean*; Robert Rosenfeld for his advice on book publishing; Rosa Smith-Montanaro for her book publishing guidance; Samantha Tassone, my business partner in Human Capital Strategy Partners; Kelly Tovar Mullaney for her help with social media and marketing; Keith Trammel for his book jacket photograph; Tom Traub for his indefatigable support and taking my book to Europe and the Middle East; Mike Waters for his sage advice; Diane Wiley for her patient editing and many clients and friends for their wonderful quotes, advice, and aphorisms; and many more to add as this project grows and evolves.

My parents, Zoila and Jose Luis, have been an inspiration my entire life. Their optimism, their faith in God, their abiding love and unfailing support in all aspects of my life have been invaluable.

And of course, I received constant support and affirmation from my wife, Sharon, and my children, Alison, Alexander, and Bradley. They accommodated my crazy schedule when I met with clients and patiently waited for me to get off the computer as I spent countless hours writing this book.

Luis Martínez
Pittsford, New York

INTRODUCTION

Change is my opportunity.
—LAM

A job search is a very difficult process for most people. There is so much incertitude, no clear avenues, and no definitive direction. Everything that's important to us seems to be in the hands of strangers. If unemployed, we are very uncomfortable without a job. We don't like the process of presenting ourselves to strangers and trying to persuade them to hire us. This process is very unpleasant, even for the best prepared.

There are factors that impede many people—whether frustrated in their current positions or unemployed—from being productive in their job search. One of them is that they don't know how to go about it. Another one is fear.

If you feel you don't have the tools necessary for an effective job search, or if you fear the process of getting started toward a meaningful career, then I think you'll find the steps outlined in this book and should help you in your job search by:

a. Outlining some basic concepts to quickly launch your job search and then,
b. Providing a tool kit (strategies and tactics) with easy-to-follow directions to improve your confidence and reduce your fear of being unprepared.

As I meet with many clients who have used the process presented in this book, they have all marveled at how easy the concepts are to learn, and how quickly they can turn one or two hours of good work with these tools into a solid, productive job search process with excellent results.

Over the years, I have purchased and read a not small number of the most popular career-counseling and job-search books. Perusing them, I have asked myself, "If I were unemployed, and my wife and children and other dependents were waiting to see my plan for finding work, which of these multihundred-page books would I buy, and where would I begin?"

Well, the fact that you have this book in hand makes it easy to answer that question. Begin right here on this page and follow along in the order presented. Read and do everything required in Career Coaching 101 (CC-101). When you're satisfied that you've completed the homework assignment for CC-101, then read and do the required homework for the rest of the chapters.

> *I read your book in just a few hours, while I was having my car*
> *serviced. Then I went home and started working with it.*
> —James W. Grunert, Human Resources executive

Even if you don't finish the book, you'll be prepared to approach targeted companies and successfully interview with them as long as you finish the homework in CC-101 through CC-103, at least.

After coaching hundreds of people, I can say that all of my clients who have done the work required in CC-101, 102, and 103 have found the following:

- They are focused on what they really want, what they love to do, and have shelved all other distracting, nonproductive pursuits and time-wasting activities.
- They have more confidence in the tools—"elevator speech," resumé, and cover letter—needed in order to introduce themselves to potential employers.
- They are more discerning and better able to choose among potential employers.
- They are oftentimes much better prepared for the interview than the hiring manager(s) interviewing them.
- They march with confidence toward the negotiating table for salary, benefits, and associated perquisites.
- They get all this done and move on to their new career with a better sense of effectiveness and efficiency.
- But most of all, they know they're starting to do work that they love to do.

In your job search, you can choose to sit and ponder and study and delve ever more deeply into different occupations, types of employers or geographies, or an infinite number of details about jobs or job characteristics. Some well-known books go to great lengths to help you understand your skills and experience. Others dwell to a great degree on personality types. However, if you find yourself dwelling on more and more detail, analyzing ever more data, you will quickly realize that you've run into a condition known as "the law of diminishing returns," meaning that no matter how much more detail and data you gather, and how much more you explore and drill down at these factors, the results are not significantly better.

So where do we start? I suggest you start by understanding who you are, and then move toward putting together a tool kit to define a long-term strategy supported by short-term tactics as you build your next career.

This, in short, is the thesis of this book—you need to start with a thorough understanding of *who you are.*

If you are introspective and know something about yourself, then you can prepare an effective job search campaign. Conversely, if you don't know yourself sufficiently, your resume and other job search tools may lead you in the wrong direction, and your efforts may result in another miserable job.

An analogy that we can use is sports car racing. Preparing for a race requires a strategy, planning, and many tactics. An expert driver with an unsorted, untried car, which has not been shaken down for peak performance, will have difficulty finishing the race. Likewise, the best-prepared car, completely prepared mechanically and dynamically for a particular race circuit, will have a low probability of finishing, let alone winning, with a rookie or inexperienced driver.

As the driver, you have to understand the capabilities and limits of your talent. You must also have a thorough understanding of the capabilities of your race car. Understanding both is necessary for optimal results.

This concept of strategizing, planning your work and then working your plan, carrying out and executing your tactics is also true in career decision making. In this instance, you are the driver; but no matter how skilled or experienced you are, you must first plan and prepare for your race. You will need a strategy for the main event. You will need some trusted advisors and helpers (pit crew members), some thorough preparation of your materials and tactics, and some practice laps.

On the Human Condition

One morning I walked into my neighborhood coffee shop and asked for my usual—a double espresso in a demi tasse. As I waited for my espresso, I noticed that my coffee server friend, Tina Francis,* looked upset. When I got her attention, she took her rest break, came out from behind the counter, hugged me tightly, and cried on my shoulder.

Tina, what's the problem? Why are you so upset?

They distributed all the weekly tip money yesterday, and I was counting on receiving $44, but they didn't save any for me. Now my bank account is going to be short! I don't have anywhere to turn, I'm short forty-four dollars! My checks will bounce!

Look, Tina, first of all, I'll help you . . .

Don't you dare! I won't accept it from you!

Okay, we'll get to that later, tell me what's happened?

I then just sat quietly next to Tina, letting her explain.

They don't get me, these young people who work here, we can't relate to each other. I'm only doing this coffee shop thing until I can find my own career again. For them working here, it's just to make some spending money. But to me, right now, it's my life! This is all I am!

Tina had been a six-figure marketing executive consultant who had offices overseas. She had made a lot of money working with major pharmaceutical enterprises, so she invested it and created a business. But the market for her services had gone into a deep downward spiral in the economic downturn of 2009. She eventually retreated to her hometown and settled for a server position in a local coffee shop in order to have access to a health care plan, a small salary and some tip money. As she explained her predicament, how she got to this level, how far she had dropped economically, she seemed in despair. She then related how very hard it is to come down so far, so fast, while the young people around her don't understand, can't understand.

Just then, the manager came forward and gave her the $44 tip money. Evidently there had been a mistake. Someone had erroneously picked up her tip money and returned it.

It was a great relief for Tina, momentarily—this instant. But the struggle would not cease. Tomorrow she would hope that her car would not break, that she would not be facing any unplanned expenses with her very small income.

Tina then composed herself and turned her attention to her computer, looking for people to meet, for positions to apply for, looking for hope.

[NB: The incident described could have happened anywhere. This is a story about the human condition during extraordinarily difficult economic times.]

Are you ready to change?

There are a number of potential obstacles in your path to a better career. The most daunting of them will be your ability to make a change. There is a vast amount of empirical data demonstrating that individuals and organizations are highly resistant to change. For example if a person is shown hard data that if they don't change the way they live, they will certainly die an early death, what are the odds that the person will change their habits? How likely is it that they will change their way of life when faced with irrefutable evidence that they must change or perish? The odds that the person will *not* change are nine to one. That's right—in the context of heart disease and its consequences—rational people will consistently resist making changes in their diet, exercise and smoking habits, and continue on a path where they will suffer debilitation, discomfort, and early death (Alan Deutschman, *Change or Die*, 2007).

The purpose of this section is not to frighten you, but to present this phenomenon, have you face it, understand it, and take action for positive change. It's important to keep this in mind—that change is necessary—and that the process of *making a decision and implementing effective change is, in fact, your greatest obstacle.* All other obstacles have a work-around; they are all subject to tactical approaches that have a probability of achieving success. Every diet works—if you follow it. Every fitness program works—if you exercise. And many aspects of this and other career and life-coaching books will work—if you implement the suggestions. But they all require your willingness to make a change.

> *Change is easy to propose, hard to implement and extraordinarily*
> *difficult to maintain.*
> —Hargreaves and Fink (2006)

Right now, before you read the next line, decide to make a change for the better!

Good. Now we can proceed.

My Agenda

My agenda is very simple. I love to help people with their careers. What I hope you get out of this book is a number of strategies and tactics that will assist you with the entire job search process, end to end, and do so quickly and effectively without encountering the dreaded and time-wasting condition of diminishing returns.

Here's how one of my clients reacted a few years ago, after our first meeting, to learn about my career coaching process:

Luis, you were the best thing that happened to me all last week.

Tara, what are you talking about? What do you mean by that?

All I have at home are my kids screaming, I can't find a job, I'm behind on my bills, I have creditors knocking at my door threatening repossession. My husband's not doing anything, he's not any help. It's just chaos at home.

Oh, Tara, I'm so sorry things are so bad. But all we did was discuss what you love to do, your attributes, and how you can start your job search. It's just tools.

No—it was hope.

Tara Whitman[1] during our second meeting

---

[1] Names denoted with an asterisk are fictitious to protect the privacy of my clients, but their stories are true exactly as depicted, with their permission.

ONE

CAREER COACHING 101

Who Are You?

Fundamentals

Begin where you are. Begin now.
—Dr. Norman Vincent Peale, minister/author

Typically, when someone starts looking for work, they think of a company that they'd like to work for. "Oh, I hear that Johnson & Johnson is a great place to work." Or, "I have a friend who works in J. P. Morgan Chase, and she really likes it there." Or, "As a schoolteacher, my first preference would be to work in suburban school district."

That's understandable—imagining ourselves in a workplace that appears to meet our needs. In fact, there are many books and articles available that promote that very notion—"the best 100 companies to work for" or "the top 100 fastest-growing careers." Many who approach their job search in this manner in fact succeed, that is, they get a top 100 job in their workplace of first choice, only to find out months later that they've made a big mistake. How does that happen?

It happens because they went about it from the outside in—instead of from the inside out.

Think about what happens when you drop a pebble in a pond. The nucleus of the activity is where the pebble strikes the water. From that point, concentric circles form and travel outward in all directions. Similarly, the first step in your career search is to understand yourself as the nucleus, the center point and source of the activity. Who are you—in a professional sense?

Some of the questions that you must ask yourself are these: What interests you? What compels you to action? What sort of activities do you enjoy? What do you love to do?

> *Identify your passion in life—what kind of work would you do, for little or no pay, because you just love doing it.*
> —LAM

Interests

Okay, let's go to work. Focus on your *interests*, not jobs or positions. Think introspectively about the sort of person that you are. Knowing who you are will help define the kind of places where you would want (or not want) to work. Remember the pebble in the water—that's you at your core, with your favorite activities, your talents displayed, and your *attributes* demonstrated (more on this later).

Think of what you *love to do*, the *skills* necessary to do it, and your *attributes*.

Discovering What You Love to Do

> *You've got to find what you love.*
> —Steve Jobs, founder Apple, Inc., NeXT, and Pixar

Surely you have sat and wondered what it would be like doing a job that you love to do—and getting paid for it. You may have sat with a cup of coffee during a nice afternoon in your family room and thought, *Why can't I find a job where I can be really happy?* After careful consideration, you may have deemed that to be an unachievable dream, and then, with a deep sigh, you settle for your current condition.

Well, it's time to turn that dream into reality.

With this book I want to help you by asking you to read and record, to read and write your responses to various easy questions found in the homework sections at the end of the first few chapters. If you do this, then you will see tangible results quickly. Follow this process, and by the time you finish the first chapter, you'll have some tools in hand. By the end of the second chapter, you'll be ready to write to companies and request interviews. By the end of the third chapter, if you have done the homework, then you'll go to interviews and come across very impressively to your hiring manager.

That should be sufficient by way of introduction. Let's begin work right now.

ATTENTION: THIS IS THE MOST IMPORTANT THING IN THIS BOOK THAT YOU WILL DO TO HELP YOURSELF!

- Sit down with a pen and a paper and think about a time in a particular job when you loved what you were doing:

  o *What* were you doing, specifically?

  o *Where* were you?

  o Who were the *people involved?*

  o *Why is it precisely that you loved this activity?* Some examples: You love selling jewelry at Lord & Taylor because you really enjoy the smiles of the customers when they purchase a piece. Or you love personal training because you see the progress that your clients are making with weight loss, healthier eating habits, and physical fitness. Or you love closing a multimillion-dollar deal because of the challenges of the complexity, the intellect of the parties involved, and the sweet rewards of a large commission. You can write about whatever you love to do: gardening, leading corporate tax strategy, coaching basketball, analyzing actuarial trends, drawing comic figures, designing offshore petroleum drilling platforms, breeding pedigreed Labrador retrievers, etc. The activity doesn't matter as long as you write in *complete sentences*, explaining *why you love this particular activity*, in great detail.

  o *What are your skills, your strengths?* Many career-counseling guides place emphasis on skills. It's a safe bet that if you have strengths, in say, organization, coordination, and social/interpersonal skills, it's easy for you love to work as an events planner. If you want a comprehensive answer to this question, then it's good practice to share your notes with a few people who know you, and ask them if you've missed any.

  o *What behaviors do you see in yourself* that make you believe you are good at what you do? Again, after you list your own responses, share your data with a few trusted friends. They will help you.

  o *Which results or positive outcomes* in your work experience demonstrate that you're good at what you're doing? You should be able to easily quantify good outcomes, for example: "Increased sales for my company by significant sums when I redesigned their approach to ethnic markets."

- Make sure you think about and enumerate those things that you *don't* enjoy.

  o *Understanding what you're not good at*, or does not make you happy, is just as important as what you love to do. If you love to work on teams, you'll be unhappy in a back office in a cubicle by yourself. However, if you can't concentrate with people walking in and interrupting your thought process, then you'll be more productive in a back office in a cubicle by yourself.

  o *Surveying work environments* is easily done by perusing business publications. Chances are that if you are intelligent and well educated, you can land many types of positions, including positions that are wrong for you, positions that you regret later unless you have clearly defined them as careers you will not pursue. But even when you have selected an industry sector, you have to be very discerning. For example, you could decide that you would love working for a retailer, but which type of retailer—Walmart or Neiman Marcus? Home Depot or Barnes & Noble? Sears or Johnston & Murphy? Piggly Wiggly or Whole Foods?

- This process of defining exactly what you love to do *is a lot like writing a letter to a trusted friend.*
- Many clients, when asked to do this type of introspection, will respond, "Gee, I have never thought about it. This is hard. *Where do I start?*"
- Start by pretending you are telling your best friend about those things you love to do. *Pretend you're writing a letter* to your old high school or college friend and you want to tell them how you're doing, in terms of work—what you love to do, where you've been most successful and most satisfied.
- *Do not constrain yourself!* This is not the time to think, "Well, I've always loved to cook, and everyone loves my gourmet dishes, but I shouldn't begin by saying I love to cook. That's not really important." Well, actually that is *most* important because what follows is the question, *Why* do you love to cook? Then, many a client will enthusiastically answer this question by saying, "Oh, I love *researching* new recipes, *making* a shopping list, *inviting* some friends over for a dinner, *organizing* all the ingredients, *coordinating* all the different dishes, *managing* the kitchen while my guests are socializing, thinking of *creative* ways to present the meal, *exploring* different wine pairings, *consuming* the great repast with my friends, and finally, *accepting* all the compliments when it all *results* in a great dining experience for them." It's obvious from this

brief interchange that cooking is very important to this person, and that it takes a significant amount of work and coordination to create a dining experience. So the importance lies in the fact that this is the foundation for the type of work this person would like—work that involves initiative, research, exploration, creativity, problem solving, coordination, timing, socializing, and event management. But look! You thought she was just *cooking*.

- By definition, *hobbies are activities that we enjoy for their own sake*. Rarely do they yield any income. (My hobby, sports car racing, *requires* a cash inflow! The joke goes, "How do you become a millionaire? Easy, start out as a billionaire and go racing.") All hobbies—volunteer work, coaching children's sports, community work—all such activities are significant indicators of (a) what we love to do, *pro bono*, and (b) what we're instinctively good at doing.

- While you're writing down what you love to do, it's not enough to say, "I like working with people." Or, "I like numbers." Or, "I like project management." *You need to clarify your ideal work situation*; you need to *visualize* your dream job (more on visualization later).

- In your attempt to catalog what you like, *you need to be very specific*. (You should also know what you don't like.) If you like working with numbers, is it because you like solving mathematical problems, as in engineering, or entering debits and credits on ledgers as in accounting? Is it doing regression analysis of compensation data, or is it decoding enemy-coded messages? If you like working with people, do you mean as a physician, as a retail sales clerk, or as a member of the clergy? And even within those categories, there are other subcategories which can be derived. You can be highly specialized; for example, you may love working as lay clergy with incarcerated pregnant women.

Environments

Shop for culture.
—Denise Johnson, Human Resources, GE Capital

As you make your list of what you love to do, you should think about the types of environments (not companies) where you would love to work. *Every work environment has a culture.* What type of culture would you love to work in? Even in a midsized city, there are hundreds of potential work settings that you could approach. How do you differentiate? Where do you start?

Start with environments. What sorts of physical spaces appeal to you? By that I mean, can you picture yourself working in a law firm? Would you be interested in the residential home construction industry? What about a senior management position in retail department stores? Would a multinational manufacturing conglomerate be appealing to you?

Those are different environments. It's just as important to know what you want (say, architectural firms), as what you don't want (emergency room administration).

Envision the types of *environments* where you would be comfortable working. Even the same genre can take many forms, for example:

- *Construction sites, outdoors*—wearing hard hat and boots, clearing land for excavating sites, supervising, surveying for commercial property, civil engineering projects, and offshore rig construction.
- *Construction sites, indoors*—project management, residential construction, building inspection, safety investigation for subsidized community projects.
- *Retail*—local restaurant chain, high-end boutique jewelry, hardware "big box" depot, luxury leather goods.
- *Academic*—private, expensive, exclusive preparatory school; downtown public school; marine research laboratory; medical college or teaching hospital.
- *Legal*—three-person practice, fifty-person practice, Legal Aid Society, corporate in-house counsel.
- *Health care*—rural public health, hospice care, coronary intensive care, nursing school faculty.

The point is that the more specific you are about the activities that you love to do, the better you will understand what kinds of positions you will, or will not, pursue.

But what's that you say, you still don't know what you want? Let's try visualization to approximate a response to this question—and more importantly, enable improvements in your work life.

Here is how you begin to explore this most important aspect of your job search and find an answer for yourself.

The next step is of crucial importance to help yourself. Turn toward the back of this book and use attachment A to write down specific activities that you love to do, for example (these are real examples from actual clients):

o Presenting complex information technology solutions to clients.
o Developing corporate strategy for markets in the Pacific Rim.
o Teaching piano.

o   Purchasing raw materials by the trainload.
o   Organizing large complex conventions in Las Vegas.
o   Keeping books and finance ledgers for restaurants.
o   Investing pension assets.
o   Creating marketing collaterals for a shipping conglomerate.
o   Writing software for medical robotics.
o   Recruiting nurses.
o   Conducting safety inspections of hospital build sites.
o   Fund-raising for cancer research.
o   Managing strategic finances for a mattress manufacturer.

Make sure you write in *complete sentences*, including the specific reasons *why* you love doing this activity.

This is crucial.

The whole point is to understand *why* you love to do certain things. If you just write "sales" or "teaching" or "accounting," you will not have captured the fundamental, intrinsic incentives that are inherent for you in doing that activity.

Write complete sentences like this: "I love speech therapy because I can see the progress the patient makes from deficits in oral communication to a fully functioning person, so then they can move on with their life in a healthy, complete way."

Maybe you like to work alone. "I love to work from home, writing software, because my children are off to school, I have everything I need nearby, I can take care of the phone and e-mail on my own timing, and no one is coming around my office to bother me with chitchat and wasting my time."

Or, "I love selling expensive yachts because I love to be near those magnificent machines on the water, I love the intelligence of the buyers, the fact that they've been very successful in their businesses, and with them I have to assemble very complex deals and bring them to closure. Then I love to get invited for a ride in their new yacht."

Deal Busters

You must also be cognizant and understand those things that are deal breakers for you. Maybe one consideration as you look for work is that you need flexibility to run errands for an ailing parent. Or maybe you do your best work at 2:00 a.m., so you need the ability to take a laptop home to do your work and deliver your best results by noon the next day. Another example: if you are bored with just maintaining current-state processes or so-called legacy systems, then older, mature companies will likely be boring for you because they typically have many legacy systems that need constant backup and support, often with obsolete hardware and software. If you are bored with the routine of maintaining old systems, then it's important for you to understand the answer to this question: Is the company you have in mind still growing and evolving? Does it have the technology, business problem, or technical challenges that excite you? Or is it old, mature in its business sector, with little prospect for growth?

If it's a multinational company you are eyeing, make sure you understand whether you can travel overseas. If the location is far from home, how long a commute you can handle and still coach your son's soccer team? If the organization is open 24-7, such as a hospital, discuss with your family whether you can work weekends or work the second shift, etc.

In other words, if you write down and understand your specific needs and constraints, then you are more likely to focus on the type of environment where you'll be most successful.

It is just as important to *rule out* environments, as to list those that are appealing.

Recognizing and Recording Your Skills

Let's return to attachment A. In your schooling and in your work experience, you have acquired job-related skills. Some are very tangible, e.g., repairing truck diesel engines; others are less tangible such as customer relationship management. Sit down and make a list: what skills have you learned that you are qualified to do?

> *Skills are those things you have learned which you can teach to others or*
> *you can turn into cash!*
> —LAM

Write down as many skills as you can think of in attachment A. These are some examples from among my clients:

o   Personal computing, e.g., Microsoft Office Suite, Access database management, etc.
o   Sarbanes-Oxley expert, global pharmaceutical
o   Marketing, luxury jewelry
o   Tax auditing, national health care
o   Guidance counseling, elementary schools
o   High-speed process engineering, packaged foods

- o Web development, furniture brokerage
- o Six Sigma Black Belt, health care
- o Electrician, commercial
- o Certified project manager, insurance
- o Sous chef, French cuisine
- o Brand management, sports drink industry
- o Social media marketing, national retail
- o Certified Home Health Aide, pediatrics
- o Customer service representative, airlines
- o Administrative assistant, banking
- o Investor relations, global conglomerate

Job-related skills, such as the ones listed above, are often learned via traditional schooling and professional and academic credentialing. They are a critical component of your professional life. List as many as you can, but don't stop there.

When recording your skills, don't forget to list skills that you have developed, which you are doing outside your normal work hours. For example:

- o Martial arts instructor
- o Basketball coach
- o Emergency medical technician
- o Ski patrol
- o Volunteer firefighter
- o Sign language interpreter
- o Church treasurer
- o Literacy volunteer
- o Magician
- o Dance instructor
- o Poet
- o Teacher of English as a foreign language (TOEFL)
- o Sports car racer

Why are these hobbies relevant, you ask? Because they are born of your love for certain activities, aspects of which sometimes (not always) can be a source of gratification and satisfaction in the job as well. They invariably point to your interests, your proclivities, your areas of heartfelt dedication.

In fact, the more "your heart is in it," the more you are likely to be successful at this chosen activity.

Pardon my passion.
—LAM

By the way, I make no apologies for bringing the words *love* and *passion* and *heart* into this discussion. Mine is not some softheaded, bleeding-heart approach to life. On the contrary, read "About the Author" on the back flap of the jacket of this book, and you'll see that my life experiences have been anything but soft.

NB: At the time that I was writing the manuscript for the first edition of Getting There, *circa 2005, the words* love *and* passion *had not yet entered the vernacular of career topics. I'm proud to have been one of the first to advance this concept, which is now considered de rigueur.*

To continue cataloguing your interests and affinities, think about any individual with world-class accomplishments in any line of work or vocation—be it a professional golfer or a moneymaking master in Wall Street, a world-renowned chef, talk show celebrity host, or world-renowned open heart surgeon. If you sit down with them and have a frank conversation, they will soon describe their chosen work accompanied by words like *love, passion,* and *heartfelt.*

That's why it's imperative that you recognize those things for which you have passion, not just a passing interest. You must recognize them in yourself and allow them to be manifested in your *primal interests.* Once those are understood, then you are now in good position to select your career.

Recognize *Interests*—Don't Settle for Positions

Interests (born of)	Positions (governed by)
Love to do—those things that we would do for free, if we were independently wealthy.	**Title/company/status**—those glittering objects of pride or desire, which soothe our ego and impress the neighbors, but are not tied directly to our core values.
Values—the way we view the world, our core guiding principles.	**Short-term exigencies, pressures**—bills to pay, career ladders to climb, need to impress the in-laws.
Aspirations—what we dreamed about as we were growing up and even into adulthood.	**Subrogated to terms and conditions**—put on the back burner, left to do when we retire, set aside while we hold a job just to make money.

Ambitious intent—healthy desires for professional growth and development.	**Succumbing to concerns, fears, constraints, avoidance**—accepting jobs out of fear of failure, constraining ourselves thinking we are not desirable or believable, avoiding choices that require some front-end work for a more rewarding future.
Talents—what we were good at before we went to school.	**Schooled skills**—always necessary but not always sufficient, subject to technological changes and economic turns.
Attributes—who we are, the reason we are loved—or not loved.	**Work experience**—learned skills and knowledge as practiced over time, experiences in certain situations that are likely to reoccur in workplaces, wisdom as related to operational activities.

As I was working with a client one morning, explaining the contents and implications of the chart above, he said, "It's really about courage." He went on to point out to me that when one is unemployed or unhappy at work, one may jump into the first thing that comes along, the first opportunity, trying all the while to reconcile aspects of the new position with our values, with our criteria.

His point was that we should have the *courage to hold fast to our values and criteria* and not just drop into the first suboptimal position that comes along, from which we will soon want to extricate ourselves.

Who Are You?

We have been discussing skills, experience, desired environments, and even values. It's very important to understand and catalogue those items about yourself before embarking on a job search. But there is something even more fundamental, without which your efforts will be misdirected and counterproductive. That something is the self—the professional self. Here's but one illustration.

Belinda Borallo* had been working for twenty-one years as an information technology global director at a Fortune 500 company. She had been putting in twelve to fourteen hours each day, plus being on call nights and weekends. Since her position was global in scope, Belinda had to accept and return phone calls at all hours, day and night, from the opposite side of the world. She had not taken a vacation in all those years. She was contemplating leaving, looking for something different to do with her career.

We met Belinda at a restaurant in Miami together with her two best friends, Peggy and Elizabeth. I started an informal CC-101 discussion with her, and I asked her to tell me about herself. She told me about her birthplace, Costa Rica, her loyalty to her current company, her family, even her dog. So I asked,

> *Okay, Belinda, that's all fine, but frankly it's not very relevant to a potential employer. So what can you tell me about your professional self?*

Her two friends agreed with me and encouraged her to discuss her values, motives, her perspectives. She then continued with how she was very loyal to her family, friends, and current employer and how hard her parents had struggled to provide for the family and how hard she had worked to gain a master's degree, etc.

I tried one more time.

> *Belinda, you have skills, experience and attributes, and personal characteristics. Let's start there, with the attributes. Tell me about yourself, the kind of person you are.*

She then told us about her employer's business processes, why some IT infrastructures worked and others didn't, how much she knew about each, and so on.

So I interrupted her softly; I touched her hand and asked,

> *Belinda, who are you?*

Her two friends laughed in sympathy.
She didn't know.

> *It's hard to read the label—when you're inside the bottle.*
> —Chuck Mefford, advertising consultant

It was obvious to all, who stood outside Belinda's bottle, that she could not read her own label; she didn't recognize herself, professionally, as others saw her.

I said to Belinda,

> *Well, I usually don't go to this level of psychological inquiry in Career Coaching 101, but I feel we must, if you are to make any progress.*

Belinda, it appears to me that you have been working so very hard for your current employer, over such a long time that although you know your personal work history, you have not had time for introspection. You have not really examined yourself, and you appear unable to answer questions about your core beliefs, your persona, your perspectives, your values and life experiences, other than those that manifest themselves at work. I'm not saying this to you in judgment. It is said with all the love and care that one can convey in a situation like this. Belinda, this is a golden opportunity to define yourself at your core. Think about it. You don't owe me an answer. I just ask that you go and discuss this with your trusted advisors. Let me know on another day, if you'd like to explore this any further.

Belinda and I continued the conversation in the restaurant, and she mentioned that she was thinking about putting down $100,000 for a franchise business opportunity. The hair stood up on the back of my neck. I said,

Belinda, just a few minutes ago we were discussing the fact that you have not had an introspective moment in over twenty years, and now you're giving serious thought to writing a check for $100,000 for a franchise, even though you don't know if you have the attributes for managing a high-pressure business. The problems of running a business are daunting, even for an experienced entrepreneur. Please, surround yourself with people you trust and discuss who you are, not the pros and cons of a franchise. You're not there yet. You will know when you're ready for that.

Peggy and Elizabeth emphatically agreed.

Belinda then said that she had been approached by another company, which asked if she would consider doing some process improvement work for them. Now, that sounded much better, if only because there was no front-end investment capital required.

I had learned a number of things about Belinda in a few hours of conversation, and I had the advantage of her two friends who were very helpful. The way we left it was that she would consider a consulting assignment for business process improvement.

Belinda and I circled back and continued with CC-101 by telephone and e-mail. As of this edition, Belinda was pursuing two opportunities. The one she was interested in was at a technology enterprise with headquarters in Miami. She has had five interviews with top managers, including their chief financial officer. She expects an offer from them. Belinda was also considered by a beverage company based in Atlanta. She interviewed with their chief talent officer and is set to return to meet other members of the management team. Both positions have similar breadth and scope, and she would not be adverse to relocation.

Some weeks later, in an e-mail from Belinda, she informed me that as a result of our conversation on that evening at the restaurant in Miami, she had learned about herself. She wrote that she was now cognizant that her answers revealed that she had not dedicated sufficient time to important things in her life. As a result of our conversation and after reading a draft of this book, she now understands that she has to improve in this respect. She then proceeded to provide examples of the steps she had taken.

By the way, Belinda mentioned that she prepared for those interviews by employing the concepts and T-chart for interviewing, outlined in CC-103—Interviews, and that she found them to be very valuable.

The main point of this anecdote is to underline the need for self-assessment, for introspection and understanding of self *prior* to even a review of the resume.

A resume built on job experience alone is a house built on sand. Before reviewing job search tools like the cover letter and resume, you must have a thorough understanding of self, at least of those aspects that affect your professional life. By doing so, you are building a platform for yourself, a platform made up of your values, attributes, and personal characteristics that will—more than anything else—be predictive of your professional success.

On the Importance of Attributes

Attribute: noun, a characteristic or quality of a person or thing (*Webster's New World College Dictionary*).

How do Attributes Make a Difference?
Suppose that Danny Wegman (who owns the renowned chain of supermarkets—Wegmans) needs to hire a pharmacist for one of his seventy supermarkets. In this hypothetical example, Danny would put a help wanted ad in the newspaper and about ten pharmacists might come forward. How will Danny decide from among them?

- All of them are qualified, e.g., by definition, a pharmacist is working in a credentialed "closed" profession with a license and documented skill set.
- Let's assume that all of the candidates love their work, more or less.
- Let's assume also that they are similarly well situated, vis-à-vis their skills and overall work experience.

- No one clearly stands out above the others in these categories.
- All of them, therefore, have what I call competent resumes. How will Danny Wegman make a choice?

Have you heard hiring managers say this: "I hired Denise on instinct." Or, "There was good chemistry between us, so that's why I chose Greg." Or, "After looking at everyone's skills and experience, my gut told me that Elizabeth was the right person for the job."

What are they talking about? What do they mean by instinct? Gut? Chemistry?

They are referring to *attributes*—the candidate's personal attributes. That is, whether the person seems to be compassionate, enthusiastic, detail-minded, extroverted, organized, driven, shy, pugnacious, humorous, inscrutable, etc. (see a partial list of attributes in the appendix).

We all unconsciously look for certain attributes when we meet people. In hiring situations, whether we realize it or not, we try to discern those attributes that we think are commensurate with ours or with our needs even if we can't articulate what they are.

My contention is that *it's your attributes, not your skills, which are the best predictors of your success.* Even the best qualified applicant, in terms of skills and experience, can fail if their attributes are not a match for the employer's stated or nonstated requirements. That's why it is so important that you understand who you are and demonstrate your personal attributes.

Many hiring managers hide behind a long list of strict skills and experience requirements while ignoring vastly better candidates because they are afraid of basing their decision on the most fundamental of human interactions—our instincts about attributes.

But the best recruiters or hiring managers are adept at finding those attributes that are needed in any given hiring situation, and they use their interviewing and screening experience to bring them out in the candidate. Those recruiters and hiring managers have much better outcomes in their hiring decisions.

This recent article by a professional services newsletter supports my hypothesis, e.g., that personal attributes—not skills—are critical to your success in a new position:

WHY NEW HIRES FAIL. According to a study by Leadership IQ, 46 percent of newly hired employees will fail within eighteen months while only 19 percent will achieve unequivocal success. But contrary to popular belief, **technical skills are not the primary reason why new hires fail** [author's emphasis]; instead, poor interpersonal skills dominate the list, flaws which many of their managers admit were overlooked during the interview process. The study found that 26 percent of new hires fail because they can't accept feedback, 23 percent because they're unable to understand and manage emotions, 17 percent because they lack the necessary motivation to excel, 15 percent because they have the wrong temperament for the job, and only 11 percent because they lack the necessary technical skills. Eighty-two percent of managers reported that in hindsight, their interview process with these employees elicited subtle clues that they would be headed for trouble. But during the interviews, managers were too focused on other issues, too pressed for time, or lacked confidence in their interviewing abilities to heed the warning signs. "The typical interview process fixates on ensuring that new hires are technically competent," explains Mr. Mark Murphy, chief executive officer of Leadership IQ. "But coachability, emotional intelligence, motivation and temperament are much more predictive of a new hire's success or failure."

In addition, this study found no significant difference in failure rates across different interviewing approaches (e.g., behavioral, chronological, case study, etc.). However, 812 managers experienced significantly more hiring success than their peers. What differentiated their interviewing approach was their emphasis on interpersonal and motivational issues. "Highly perceptive and psychologically-savvy interviewers can assess employees' likely performance on all of these issues," explains Mr. Murphy. "But the majority of managers lack both the training to accurately read and assess candidates, and the confidence to act even when their assessments are correct. Hiring failures can be prevented," he notes. "If managers focus more of their interviewing energy on candidates' coachability, emotional intelligence, motivation and temperament, they will see vast improvements in their hiring success. Technical competence remains the most popular subject of interviews because it's easy to assess. But while technical competence is easy to assess, it's a lousy predictor of whether a newly-hired employee will succeed or fail."

Reprinted with permission from: MICHAEL D. ZINN & ASSOCIATES, INC., ®, Executive Search Newsletter, February 2006.

The best predictors of your professional success are understanding yourself and demonstrating the required attributes for your desired position.

Further evidence to the importance of attributes is in research conducted by Fali Huang and Peter Cappelli of the National Bureau of Economic Research. Their findings indicate that when employers screen applicants for the attribute work ethic, they realize greater productivity in work teams. In fact, *screening for work ethic* in their study was found to be much more effective in attracting and retaining talented staff than screening for cognitive abilities, which does not produce these positive productivity results.

One of my clients reacted this way about the importance of attributes:

For the first time in many years I feel lifted up and, for the lack of a better word, understood. You are the first person to tell me not to restrict my personal attributes (likes and dislikes) in order to find a job, but rather build upon them. For so many years I felt that I had to conform and adjust attributes of myself to conform to some organization. For the first time I feel it is okay to go out for what I love to do, instead of finding something that I can do. I have lost so much confidence in myself, I was without direction and felt lacking in so many departments, simply because I bought into the idea that I had to fit myself to a job—instead of finding a good match. Now, looking back, I realize that the jobs I loved most were those for which my personality/attributes were well suited, and in which I had established a good rapport with the interviewers/future supervisors almost instantaneously.

It is like you opened my eyes. I know I have a ways to go, but that is okay. Leaving this morning's meeting with you, I felt motivated, energized, and most of all, hopeful. I know it seems exaggerated to have such a reaction to a one-hour-long meeting, but that's how I feel. Thank you so much! I am truly looking forward to working with you on me.

—Gabriele Vogt, from her e-mail after our first meeting

Now, back to Danny Wegman and his search for a pharmacist. A smart hiring manager will make his or her final decision, discerning from among qualified candidates, on the *attributes* of the candidate, that is, on the candidate's demonstrated personal characteristics and how well they match the professed requirements of the hiring manager.

Here is a story of how attributes, when properly positioned, can dramatically affect the outcome of a job search.

Tara Whitman's Story

One of my clients, we'll call her Tara Whitman,* telephoned me and asked for help with her resume. Typically, that's how the conversation starts. "I'm looking for work, and I need some help with my resume." This can be done. That is, I can help someone with their resume and send them on their way.

But I'm not a resume writer. Resume building is only a fraction of the process. Indeed, the resume is a tool—and a backward looking tool, at that. The purpose and tactics of resume writing are detailed in Career Coaching 102 (CC-102). But let's come back to Tara and how the attributes mentioned in the first part of her resume made all the difference in how she was perceived by the hiring manager and the position she was offered.

Tara started out with a resume that contained all the skills and experiences of an accounting clerk, a nonexempt, seasoned, business clerical employee. Tara's original resume shows that her objective was "bookkeeper, billing clerk/collections, accounting clerk, database/Web site administrator, presentations." In my first meeting with Tara to discuss her occupational situation, I saw that she could quickly have landed a position as an accounting clerk. There is a good job market for those skills. But her pay would have been in the low twenties per year at about $10 to $12 per hour. Tara needed a better paying job in order to meet her family's financial requirements. After meeting and getting to know Tara to some degree, I pointed out that she had more going on for her than her resume indicated.

During our meeting, I recorded the personal attributes that Tara mentioned about herself. I tested these to make sure she could back them up. So for example, when she said she was results driven, I asked for stories and examples of her work, which would support her claim. I asked her for instances of how she had demonstrated attention to detail, and how she had been resourceful.

It's very important, indeed critical, that when you write down an attribute, you are able to back it up. There's no point in feigning to be sociable and outgoing when, in fact, you prefer to work alone and not have your day interrupted by people.

The results of our discussion became evident in her revised resume, where Tara indicated that she is a "results-driven, detail-oriented, enthusiastic office management professional desiring an opportunity to utilize my skills, experience, and attributes to help generate revenue and maintain customer relationships, contract administration, and process optimization for a professional services organization."

In this new "elevator speech" from Tara, where is the bookkeeper? Where is the accounts receivable clerk? She now had a much more potent resume and cover letter, yet her skills and experience were the same, just presented in a more compelling fashion with a greater emphasis on her attributes.

Tara submitted her cover letter and resume (more on the use of attributes in cover letters in CC-102), and she interviewed for a contract administrator position. This would have been a nonexempt position paying in the high $20s. But after the interview process was over, the blue chip company, Xerox Corporation, offered Tara a supervisory position, paying $55,000 a year. This was beyond Tara's wildest dreams.

What made the difference? It was positioning Tara in a way that her attributes—results-driven, problem-solving, resourceful office management professional—would be in plain view to the hiring manager and would distinguish her from the many other competent but undistinguished resumes piled high on the hiring manager's desk.

I need mirrored back to me how much I value myself.
—Lori Webster Koonmen

Soft Skills? What Soft Skills?

I guess I take umbrage at the notion that personal attributes and interpersonal skills are generally referred to as soft skills. I would dare anyone to say to Tara Whitman that her determination, resourcefulness, tenacity, and results-driven nature are soft skills. She would take issue with that, I would bet. And anyone who has had to learn to be more assertive or to become mellower or more detailed or more strategic would tell you that there is nothing soft or easy about learning and honing those characteristics. They are as difficult to master as any "hard" skill, such as writing software or studying for certified public accountant boards. Granted, they can be characterized as interpersonal skills as different from, say, clinical skills or musical skills, but referring to them as soft creates a delusion that they are somehow less important, if not irrelevant, which is definitely a counterproductive notion.

Corporate recruiters will emphasize interpersonal skills, including leadership and teamwork. Alan Breznick, of Cornell University, asserts in the university's Cornell Enterprise Johnson School of Business Magazine that "such intrinsic qualities as leadership and teamwork are difficult if not impossible to teach on the job." Recruiters must find a way to elicit these qualities from the candidates through the job interviews.

Karin Ash, director of Cornell's Johnson School Career Management Center, says, "Recruiters want candidates who can clearly articulate who they are, where they're going, and who can persuade other people around them."

From Tears to Cheers in Just Five Weeks

The only way to do great work is to love what you do.
If you haven't found it yet, keep looking.
Don't settle.
—Steve Jobs

Darlene VanSant* worked across the hall from me. One day she knocked on my office door:

Luis, do you have a minute?

Sure, Darlene, come on in, have a seat. What's up?

Luis, my manager just gave me my annual performance appraisal, and well, I've never received such a low appraisal. I am totally distraught. I did everything he asked me to do. He is so difficult to work for. And after all that, after all the nights and weekends during Christmas and New Years, he gives me a low evaluation! Now I can't even transfer out because they'll see this appraisal, and they won't want me. I'm stuck! Right at the peak of my career—I'm stuck with a manager who doesn't like me!

Darlene was in tears by now. I had observed her over the previous several weeks as she worked long hours during the holidays; she never smiled much. She seemed to be always under a lot of pressure. It did not surprise me that she was having a rough time, but now her manager had made it official—in her personnel documents.

What can I do, Luis? I'm forty-six, and I've been working my way up the corporate structure. I accepted this assignment in December, as a stepping stone, and now I've hit a rock. I don't know where to go from here. I can't believe this is happening.

Darlene, let's discuss your work history, your aspirations, your aptitudes. I love to do career coaching, I can help people in situations like yours.

You mean, you can work on my resume and stuff like that?

Well, yes, eventually we will get to revise your resume. But you've brought a larger problem to the table here, a problem that requires a lot more than a better resume. So let's get together, and I'll explain my process, and we can go one step at time.

Darlene and I met during the week. Following the process detailed in the early part of this chapter about writing down what you love to do in great detail, Darlene wrote down what she loved to do and compared it to her resume. It became obvious to her that she did not like what she was doing. That's when I saw the "Christmas tree" light up. This Christmas tree effect is how I describe the reaction of my clients, which is virtually universal, when they discover that what they love to do is not reflected in their resumes—that is, that they have been working for years doing something they don't like.

In Darlene's case, she was a CPA/MBA. She had been working as an accountant, financial analyst, and now division controller for over twenty years. And in one moment, she discovered that she had been slaving at something she didn't like to do.

Darlene, if you don't like accounting and finance, then why did you major in that field, and why did you go on and study for a CPA plus an MBA?

Because I knew I could always get a job.

Darlene and I met three times. My observation of the situation was that she needed a tactical plan to execute right away. She needed something different to do to get her out of the environment she was in that was crushing her spirit.

She also needed a strategic plan—a long-range plan that would encompass what she loves to do in a productive, financially, and emotionally rewarding way—a plan where she would eventually be able to do exactly what she loved to do.

We listed Darlene's attributes; she wrote her elevator speech and applied it to her resume. In her revised resume, Darlene answered the "So what?" questions (more on this later). She composed her cover letter and sent it to a manager within the company who had a vacancy in financial analysis.

Darlene was called for interviews. She used the T-chart for interviewing (from CC-103) and was called again for wrap-up. She was offered an internal transfer with a promotional increase. Darlene called me to her office and showed me the offer letter. She said,

This can't be true, this can't be right, because I've been in this job less than six months, and they're offering me a promotional increase. There must be a mistake.

I replied,

> *Darlene, do you see the signatures on this offer letter? They are from the corporate office. This came from Connecticut. This has the highest authority. There's nothing wrong with this offer. Think it over.*

Darlene signed the offer. She started in her new job in only five weeks after she had first come into my office.

She invited me out to lunch to celebrate her promotion. Now, to put this in context, Darlene is a very conservatively dressed, very restrained individual who measures her words carefully and is not given to displaying her emotions. While discussing these events over lunch at the restaurant, Darlene looked me in the eye and said,

> *Luis, I was meant to transfer to your building in December. I was meant to meet you. You were meant to be there during the time of my professional crisis. This was meant to happen exactly this way. This was supposed to happen!*

I was surprised at her:

> *Darlene, are you sure you're okay? Why, I've never heard you say things like this. Listen to what you're saying. The things you are saying are very spiritual.*

> *Luis, I'm sure of it, this was meant to happen.*

But wait; there's more.

I continued meeting with Darlene now and then; we would meet and she'd tell me how she was doing in her new job. Her job was now much more congruent with what she loved to do. But it was still incomplete. There was something still missing. She had decided, as a result of our many discussions, that what she really wanted to do was to be the chief financial officer of a not-for-profit organization. With that concept in mind, we laid out a strategy. Darlene was patient as she planned her work and worked her plan to perfection. One Friday she received the layoff notice she had been expecting from her employer, complete with a very generous severance package, and the following Monday she was working as the CFO of a not-for-profit organization.

We are not human beings having a spiritual experience; we are
spiritual beings having a human experience.
—Pierre Teilhard de Chardin

Values

Parallel and closely related to our attributes are our values. Yes, you have values, we all do. This is our religion—the way we see the world.

It is important to model your values in your work as well as in your personal life. Career decisions should be based on some personal, deeply held view of the world.

- Get in touch with your values, those principles you hold dear.
- Discuss your values with a trusted advisor.
- Make a brief list of your values and validate each.
- With values in hand, look at *environments* first, not companies—the types of businesses you may/may not want to work in. For example, the insurance industry, the construction industry, commercial real estate, health care, hospitality, not-for-profit, higher education, finance, etc., are environments.
- After you have decided what environments you may want to work in, for example: banking or corporate law or public administration, then you can learn about companies within those environments—their cultures, stated and realized values, and policies.
- It's also important to know what you *don't* want—so be prepared to discard the whole:

  o environments,
  o industries, and
  o companies.

Find something you love to do, and you'll never have to work a day in
your life!
—Harvey McKay, author

Generating Options

Let's think creatively about career aspirations. Here are some possible approaches and alternative avenues—using a "blue sky" approach:

- Think about many options.

o   Ask "Why?" (something is the way it is).
o   Ask "Why not?" (try something different, outside the norm).

Defining your Personal Value Proposition

I've discovered some problems that are often found among those frustrated in their careers. Let's begin to tackle a short list:

* Number 1 problem: Are you too hard on yourself?
* Number 2 problem: Do you have unrecognized/unappreciated talent(s)?
* Number 3 problem: Are you settling too quickly, escaping current reality for any quick landing?

Being too hard on oneself is a problem I find more often among women than men. Yes, there are some issues which manifest themselves more often in one gender than the other. Some women have started a career, then get married, stay at home for several years to raise their children, and then decide to reenter the workforce. They are often hesitant and don't know where to begin, as they have lost touch with their profession. They often say that they "haven't done anything all these years" and have very low expectation of themselves, which is instantly transmitted to others.

Fortunately, nowadays you can use the Internet to search topics, read many articles and topics to come up to speed on many trends and current events. You can also find professional associations and networking groups in your community so you can meet with your professional peers and uncover opportunities (read more about this in the section on networking in chapter 6). Overall, the best suggestion I can offer if you are reentering your profession, indeed, if you are unemployed or looking for a promotional opportunity is to identify a community of practice, that is, a group of people who are interested in the same things that you do. And if you can't find one, organize one yourself! More on this in chapter 6.

Other times you may find that your talents or skills are not appreciated. Indeed, you may not know yourself how you add value. But this is critically important. I refer to this professional value as your Personal Value Proposition. Your PVP is that unique combination of your skills, knowledge, and attributes, which is a solution to someone's business problems. This is why the process described above, identifying what you love to do, plus your learned skills and defining attributes is so important. The first person that has to recognize your PVP is you. Once you recognize your own PVP, then the process shifts to how to convey that to others, specifically to recruiters and hiring managers. But admittedly we all need help with this. Why? Because it's hard to see your own brand.

In your quest to identify your PVP, you will have to enlist a few people whom you know and trust or engage a career coach so they can reflect back to you those salient aspects of your professional identity. This is why relationships are so important and why networking and participating in professional associations, communities of practice, and small interest groups are pivotal. Can you really do this all by yourself? Sure. But it will take you a lot longer, you'll be frustrated, wasting time and opportunities. Ultimately, you will realize you have to associate with others to get the job done.

Take courage. Find the win-win! *You are a solution* looking for their business problem(s). Align your interests; find common threads and themes among them.

The third type of problem may be that you are settling for whatever comes by. I know some people who have told me, "I've never had to look for work, it always finds me." But when I pursue that remark and ask a few more questions, they eventually admit that they're just doing a job for the money, or for convenience, and that they'd rather be doing something else, something they love. Other examples include people who have been unemployed, or are on the verge of being laid off from a foundering enterprise, so they quickly jump to whatever is posted or advertised. Within months they regret their decision, but now say that they don't want to make a move lest they be labeled as a "jumper," someone who takes a new job every six months.

If you're not satisfied with what you are doing, or if you've been passed over for a promotion, or if you are unemployed, then *start by identifying your Personal Value Proposition*, selecting some environments that would be amenable and joining communities of practice. These steps will align you quickly to an ideal work opportunity.

As you sit down and discern your PVP, you should consider that your various career options are not mutually exclusive—consider options with apparently differing trajectories but aligning your varied interests. For example I have a good friend, Tom Garman, who works for an inbound call center of a major health care insurance company. His job affords him a steady paycheck and health and welfare benefits for his family. Tom has also been a lifelong gung fu practitioner, and he loves instructing, which is the art of sharing. He loves martial arts, and he loves sharing his knowledge. Tom took his attributes (sharing) and his skills (gung fu), and he set up a successful martial arts and self-defense studio where he covers the rent and other expenses of his hobby by charging a fee for participation.

I'm sure you can think of many others examples of those who channel their interests into hobbies where they can also make some money, usually in personal services—dance instruction, jewelry making, eBay sales, tutoring, real estate sales, interior design, etc.

Someone Will Believe in You

You may at times feel that this whole job search process is not really working, that you don't have the skills, knowledge, or attributes that will support your job search. If your unemployment benefits are about to expire, or if you're running out of time to find work or make a career change, you may feel that there is no escape. Your spouse or significant other becomes weary of your problem. Your options seem scant or nonexistent. It seems it's just you against the world.

Do not despair. If you feel this way, then here are some steps you can take:

- Offload emotion and stress with good friends, family, or a trusted advisor.

  o Find a sympathetic, objective observer.
  o Don't overload your spouse or significant other with a daily dose of your concerns; save them for the big decision.

- Suspend judgment temporarily on options (sleep on it).
- Visualize your ideal situation (more on this later).
- Have faith.

I have been there, where you are. I was unemployed for a total of fifteen months in the mid-1990s. I remember distinctly driving in my old Jeep from Philadelphia to Washington DC for a series of exploratory interviews and then walking around in my suit and necktie, carrying my briefcase through those streets in Washington, in the sweltering summer heat, saying to myself, "I need to find work. I desperately need to land a job, so I can take care of my wife and three children." Had you been there to see me, you would have seen the willpower in my face, my clenched teeth, my sheer determination. I was going to land, and it had to happen now.

But alas, it was another year before I landed. Lesson learned? Sheer doggedness and determination alone will be insufficient. They are required—but insufficient. Muscling through this process may not produce desired results.

Sometimes well-meaning people also miss the mark. I distinctly recall a well-meaning, high-fee career counselor who, while I was unemployed in 1995, asked me to come to his office for his advice and direction. When we met, he looked me very seriously in the eye and said, "Write a letter [to the executive at a company I had targeted]." He continued, "On the envelope, mark it Private and Confidential." He looked so serious, so sincere, he was really convinced that this was the ticket, that this tactic would work to get me the job. But it was the sorriest excuse for career-coaching advice I have ever received. I never went back.

Even if you follow all the suggestions in this book, you may still remain unemployed or unable to make a desired career change *on your timing*. Many things can conspire against your plans, particularly when you stake a claim that you have to find a job by such and such a time. Research done with prisoners of war demonstrates that the ones who succeeded and survived were not the ones who said, "I plan to be home, free by this date." The ones who survived to tell the story were the ones who said, "I have to get through today." So take this process one day at a time. Plan your work and work your plan, daily.

Looking back at my own history, I plotted my job search over the last twenty years and realized that I had been looking for work at precisely those times that the US economy was hobbled by very high unemployment! I not only had all the difficulties faced by anyone looking for work or making a career change; I had faced these vexing issues during eras of national unemployment rates ranging from 5.8 percent to as high as 10.1 percent while hemmed on all sides by fellow baby boomers—millions of them, all competing for precious few positions.

You may be in dire straights, but there is no need to despair. If you look around, then you will find someone who believes in you.

You have knowledge, skills, and attributes (KSAs) that someone will want so you can help them solve their business problem. In fact, even if you are lacking some of the skills and experience mentioned in the position profile, you should still be able to demonstrate attributes of importance to the hiring manager and thereby succeed in landing a good job or earn a promotion.

Here are some stories of people who believed in me and how they changed my professional life.

Porter S. Rickley

Mr. Rickley was the regional director of the US Census Bureau, Philadelphia region, when I was in my late twenties. I had been hired to do community advocacy for the national census that would take place in 1980. The census management team watched me at work, and after a few months in the job, I was asked if I would like to change career tracks from community advocacy to program supervision. I agreed to this, but I had to give up my US Civil Service exempt grade 11 and take a $3,000/year pay cut to join supervisors-in-training at grade 7. I accepted this change because it would take me out of a staff position and put me in operations, in a supervisory position. I started my training and had a lot to learn supervising survey operations.

It was Mr. Rickley who assigned me to supervise the Current Population Survey (CPS), which is the backbone of the national unemployment statistics program. I was only twenty-nine years old, and thanks to Mr. Rickley, I was trained for supervision and within a year, I was promoted to grade 9 and then later to grade 11 again. By the time I was in grade 11, I had responsibility for 142 census employees in a five-state region.

Even so, I did not recognize the significance of what Mr. Rickley had done for me until he sent me to Washington DC to attend my first national conference of CPS supervisors. It was then, faced with my counterparts from across the country, that I recognized how much he believed in me—he had assigned me to supervise their most important survey, and then I discovered that all the other CPS managers, my peers attending the conference, were US Census veterans with over twenty years' experience.

Samuel R. Huston

Sam Huston was the CEO of Lehigh Valley Hospital, the largest hospital in Pennsylvania. The task that he had been given by the board of directors was to merge two hospitals, which had historically been competitors, into one operating entity. Sam needed to fill the human resources leadership position. I responded to the search, and eventually he offered me the position. Here is where Sam differentiated himself. When he offered me the position, he asked me for my salary expectations. So I told him. Not only did he accept my salary requirements, but he raised me by $10,000. I'll never forget that phone call. Can you imagine how eager I was to start to work there?

Sam is a brilliant man. He knew how I would react to getting a raise before I started, and I had every intention of vindicating him, of making him look good for his decision to hire me. But wait, there's more. When I went to our first staff meeting with a conference room full of deans of medicine and clinical chairs and administrative leaders, there I was, the youngest again, a thirty-nine-year-old senior vice president. Sam had walked the plank for me; he believed in me, and as you can imagine, I did not disappoint.

> *Finding someone who is interested in what you have to offer—it's a lot like looking for love.*
> —LAM

I hasten to point out that neither Porter Rickley nor Sam Huston had known me previously. They were not my childhood friends or fraternity brothers or golfing buddies. So what was at play? What did they see in me?

I did not know it then, but I know it now. They saw my *attributes*. They saw my potential. I did not even have any industry experience. I did not have any experience in the census or survey administration process. And I did not have any experience in acute health care setting. Of course, there were skills and experience in corporate human resources that I could demonstrate. But more importantly, they perceived my competence and potential as conveyed by my attributes.

Someone will believe in you.

But First You Have to Believe in Yourself!

> *Stay hungry, stay foolish*
> —Stewart Brand, *The Whole Earth Catalog*

Donna Highsmith* had graduated from Fairport High School, near Rochester, New York, and earned a bachelor's degree in business administration from the Rochester Institute of Technology. Donna had been referred to me by a mutual friend in the summer of 2003. After doing all the necessary work in CC-101, she secured a position in marketing for a sports trading card company in Rochester. By 2005, she was laid off as a result of a downturn in their business. Donna called me again, and we set up a meeting to revise her paperwork and cast a new strategy. As we entered into a discussion about positions that would be desirable for her, she evidenced a deep longing to leave the cold weather of upstate New York and start a new career and lifestyle in southeast Florida.

Donna was very young but talented and determined. She had set a goal for herself to move to southeast Florida, and all she needed now was a strategy and some tactics. Reviewing her resume, I smiled saying, "This looks like the kind of resume that I have coached." And I had, just a few years before. Donna wanted to find a position in marketing, but she knew that her experience was limited. She decided to first look at a position in sales. I had no doubt, based on my meetings with Donna, that she would be a successful sales representative.

Donna stuffed her Honda Civic with as many earthly possessions as she could carry in it and drove from Rochester to Boca Raton to stay with a friend.

I remember sending her an e-mail as she embarked on her journey to Florida, saying to her, "Donna, I believe in you." This was not empty rhetoric. I knew her, as well as one could, and I firmly believed that she would achieve her objective.

Donna found a position as a sales representative with a major copier company. Armed with a steady income, she found her own place to live in Plantation, Florida, and began her career. She kept looking, however, for another job because her base salary was small and the commissions insufficient.

She applied for a position as an internal communications manager for a prominent security company. She had no experience per se in communications, but she was hired at a salary level that she wanted. How did this all take place?

I traveled to Fort Lauderdale and met with Donna for lunch. She was so proud of her accomplishments. I asked her, "Donna, you are so happy that you actually have a glow about you. Tell me, how did you get this job? Tell me about the interviews and what kinds of things they asked you."

As we had lunch, Donna talked to me about her success in landing that dream job. She said, "It was *my attributes*. They saw my energy, my enthusiasm for doing this job. I was told by the hiring manager that the other candidates did not have my attributes."

In addition to her high energy, determination, good personal interactions, and being a quick study, Donna also added that other factors were important. We discussed them and came up with a list of five major factors that were in her favor:

- First, her raw intelligence. Donna's IQ is above average, and it shows in how she approaches problems and brings solutions to bear.
- Second, her emotional intelligence. Donna displays an obvious zest for working with the human side of the enterprise, and she successfully navigated the shoals of difficult interviews.
- Third, her mother's influence and counsel. Donna credited her mother with a can-do attitude and generous optimism.
- Fourth, Donna's own life experiences. She had already experienced two layoffs. She wanted a medium-sized company, well established with a sound financial record. She had clarity and was focused on what she wanted.

- And fifth, her spiritual beliefs. Very close to Donna's optimism is a sense that if she listens to the small voice in her heart, she will do well.

What was amazing about Donna was that, mature beyond her young years, she built her plan on a solid foundation—her love for certain aspects of work, her understanding and trust that her attributes would support her, and finally her spirituality—her faith and confidence, which she used to make a decision to drive south, find a pied-à-terre, and begin a new life.

Donna had all those characteristics present when we first met. The work that I did was to hold up mirrors for Donna to see herself. What we did together was to bring out those positive characteristics, those attributes of hers, and put them on the table. We examined them objectively and built a resume, cover letters, and an interviewing strategy using my process in such a way that it would afford a hiring manager a good look at them—to Donna's eventual success.

Another client writes in her e-mail after our first meeting.

I liked the approach of the initial meeting because it was very packaged, simple to understand, and it makes the process appear much less intimidating. This approach would be especially attractive to those individuals who have been in long-term jobs and/or who really don't have a clear idea of what the next steps are. Also, for people like me who are just ready to go get to the next step and move forward!

As an action-oriented person, I liked the direct approach without a lot of fluff. It helps to focus the client on what to do next and forces them to start thinking through the written pieces that will represent themselves (cover letter/resume).

—Nancy Poisson Battles, professional recruiter

For Recent High School or College Graduates

If you have just graduated from high school or college and you have little or no experience with the work world, then the same thinking process still has value.

Think about those things you love to do that help define your attributes. What activities have you enjoyed while in school?

- Did you like organizing an overnight class trip?
- Did you enjoy being class treasurer?
- Were competitive sports your passion?

- Did you enjoy coursework in art history?
- List those activities that you enjoyed in class, especially extracurricular activities, such as writing for the school newspaper, coordinating the junior prom, acting on the school play, or participating in the debate team. Describe why you enjoyed them.
- List those job duties that you loved to do in your part-time work or summer internship: taking care of customers at a fast food concession, monitoring activities for summer camp students, working with engineers on a design proposal, organizing a computerized spreadsheet of all current vendors. Describe why you loved those duties.

Take an inventory of those things you were excited to do; make sure you detail them in your resume and cover letter (see Homework for CC-101 at the end of this chapter). Let the reader or trusted advisor see what you are good at and the reasons you think you are good at it, e.g., give examples to demonstrate your accomplishments. You will learn how to do this in the "Homework" section at the end of this chapter.

Seek and heed the advice of high school guidance counselors; also find someone in the faculty who could be a mentor. If in college, it is very likely that there is a career counseling office at your service at no additional charge. Do not wait until the spring of your senior year to make an appointment with the outplacement or career counseling office. Be sure to visit them at least once every semester or twice a year. They will help you with your resume, cover letter, interviewing skills and some drills—maybe even including video taping or mock interviews. They can also help you find paid summer internships. All of those services are part of your paid tuition, so make sure you take advantage of them.

What about the resume?

I am not a resume writer. Oftentimes, when I meet with clients, we sit down, and the first thing they do is try to show me their resume. I can see it in their eyes that they're anxious to hear my critique of their resume. "Well, how does it look?" they ask me, anxious for my quick review. They expect me to look over their resume and decide if they are adequately expressing all their skills and experience. But, frankly, I'm not ready to see their resume when we meet. I'm more interested in learning who they are.

Before I can evaluate someone's resume, I want to become better acquainted. This is what I refer to as my "clinical front end." In the early part of my coaching relationship with my clients, I want to ensure that I can effectively capture their essence; their likes and dislikes; their perspectives on work life; their relationships with their managers, peers, subordinates, and customers. I want to know from them what they consider success and failure. I'll ask them whom they admire, who has guided them, why was that guidance important to them. I'll ask them where they lived when they were happiest. I want to hear from them about their values, that is, the way they view life and the world. I have to ask them all those questions because none of those things are found in a resume.

Here's an example of what I mean. One of my dear friends, Candy, used to work in a successful career development services firm. One day she asked me to meet with her boyfriend, David, to see if I could help him with his job search. Ironically, David had already been through their career development services, but he was still frustrated, had not landed a job he could like, and in fact could not work effectively in his search. I met with David, and I asked him all my usual questions. He told me what he loved to do and all about his skills and attributes. Within forty-five minutes of our first meeting, David and I agreed that what he loved to do was to lead a small team of customer service staff. He loved leading people to achieve customer satisfaction; he loved working at establishing and maintaining excellent customer relationships. He loved training others and solving problems through a team of well-trained customer-oriented staff. David and I visualized that he would be a great customer service manager at a large retail establishment, or a large successful restaurant, or at an automobile service shop, etc. David was very excited that at last someone finally understood what he loved to do. Then I asked to see his resume. David's resume was a beautifully executed, well-spaced, and perfectly arranged resume for a diesel truck mechanic. Yes, gentle reader—for a diesel truck mechanic. What happened? It turns out that David had been, at one time, a service technician for diesel equipment in the army. The career counselor who had worked with David was a resume writer who had simply focused on his skills and experience. But the previous career counselors *had not asked him what he loved to do.* They just perfected David's resume, and now his resume reeked of where he had been.

Chapter Summary

The purpose of this section has been to encourage you to connect with your professional core, your values and aspirations—without constraints. Understanding your Personal Value Proposition, which is your unique blend of skills, knowledge, and attributes, is critically important to ascertaining your ideal position.

- Think about those things that you have *truly enjoyed*, that make you smile as you write them.

- *Do not constrain yourself* at this point! Do not say, "Well, I love to paint water colors, but there's no money in it." It's critical for you to understand why you love to paint or make cabinets or sell cosmetics or referee boxing or arrange flowers or scuba dive or fight fires or race cars. So write it down—what you love to do, and why you love to do it, no matter what it is.
- Be precise, specific on your interests. It's vital to identify what it is that moves you to do those things you love to do.
- Think deeply about why you love to do this activity—and the reason is often beyond the obvious. For example, one client said she really loved fashion design. So we explored this, and in her case it was not about dressing mannequins. What we discovered while discussing this activity is that she really loves sharing with others her interest in helping men to be well dressed, choosing among many options for clothes and accessories. She also helps men with etiquette and social graces to assist them as they socialize among affluent people who can actually afford her consulting services. This is a lot more than fashion design.
- Ask yourself "Why?" as in why you like participating in those activities—*the specific reasons you love doing certain things.* This can't be emphasized enough.
- Ask yourself "Why not?" for other activities that you have considered but not attempted.
- Look for opportunities to align differing interests with your professional choice, or use them as a platform for a personal business or service.
- In this way, by knowing and being able to verbalize your Personal Value Proposition, you will open your job search conversation with your skills and knowledge and you will close it with your attributes.

Your passion drives personal freedom and success!
—Samantha Tassone, president, Human Capital Management

Homework

1. Using the template in attachment A, list those activities within jobs that you love to do. Refer to the instructions at the beginning of this chapter. *It's critical that you write complete sentences*, explaining all your reasons, as if you're writing a letter to a friend describing those things you just love to do. Do not just write one-word answers like *accounting* or *selling*. You have to write a complete sentence, explaining *why* you

like doing that activity—what do you get out of it? What do you like about the results?

2. List all your skills in attachment A. Skills are those things that you've learned, and that you can teach others, like playing piano, litigation, merchandising, designing Web sites, supervising, customer relationship management, global purchasing, etc.

3. List your attributes in attachment A. There is a list of attributes in the appendix. Circle all those that apply. Then number your top 5 attributes, numbering them from 1 to 5, with number 1 being the highest order and number 5 the least but still very important to you.

4. Now, take out your current resume and underline in your resume all those words that appear in your list of things that you love to do. For example, if you love teaching/educating/instructing, then underline those words, but only if they appear in your resume.

5. After underlining things you love to do that you found in your resume, take a look. What do you think? Did you underline many words? Very few? What's your overall impression? Is there sufficient overlap between what you say you love to do and what you've been doing at your different jobs? Is there a large gap? *How do you feel about this comparison?*

This brings us to the end of Career Coaching 101—the most important aspect of which is for you to understand your Personal Value Proposition.

Luis,
I want to thank you for helping me re-discover my energy. In recent years
I have allowed others to drain me and I began to believe that I had lost the
drive that has brought me so far; my energy now is high and with that are
my expectations for myself both personally and professionally
—Lisa Tucker, Registered Health Information Administrator

Two

CAREER COACHING 102

The Tool Kit

The Elevator Speech

We begin with the "elevator speech" because this is manifestation of your professional identity. It is your defining label—who you are professionally. Why do we call it an elevator speech? Because it's the carefully packaged answer you would give to the question: "Tell me about yourself."

This could really happen. That is, you could find yourself in an elevator with an executive or person with the authority to hire you, or to promote you, and have need of an elevator speech.

Sounds far-fetched? Here is a true story: I was working in Philadelphia at the headquarters of Hay Associates, a prominent management consulting company. One morning, I stepped into the elevator to go up to my office on the fourth floor. A very well-dressed gentleman also stepped in. He was dressed all in black, wearing a bowler hat and carrying a very impressive black umbrella. The gentleman was none other than Dr. Milton L. Rock, who had just arrived from London. He was the managing principal of the company at the time. A very quick exchange ensued between us, and when he asked what I was doing for his company, I used my elevator speech.

What's the point? The point is that, whatever your profession—engineer, nurse, vice president for sales, global purchasing manager, chief operating officer—you should have at the tip of your tongue a brief synopsis of your KSAs: your knowledge, skills, and attributes.

What's that you say? The scenario I described is unlikely to happen to you? In fact, there may not even be any elevators in the town where you live and work! Obviously, elevators are not the reason for crafting an elevator speech. The real reason is that if you think hard about who you are, professionally, and you define it concisely, yet completely and compellingly, then you'll have a response ready for an opportunity.

The way I approach life is that everyone I encounter is deserving of my attention and respect, and everyone I encounter can become an advocate for me (and me for them . . .). Maybe you just can't greet everyone you see on your way to the subway. But certainly you can greet someone at the bus stop or at the gym or at the Little League baseball game or picnic or movie theater. Is an elevator speech appropriate at those times? Not really. But if a conversation develops and you are looking for another career opportunity, then you may want to carefully explore if that person may be in the position to connect you with someone or some opportunity. In other words, every conversation has the potential of becoming an informal job interview.

But wait, there's more. If you have an elevator speech rehearsed and ready, then that person whom you just met can become an advocate for you. Let's say that you are a marketing professional and you're trying to make a move to a more dynamic, growing enterprise. You meet someone, and they hear from you your crisp, concise, and memorable elevator speech. The objective is that if that person hears of something that you are interested in, then that person will immediately think of you and be able to say something like this, "Oh, I know someone like that. She's a marketing professional with an MBA, and she was born and educated in Venezuela so she is fully bilingual!" Now that person is your advocate.

You need advocates. That's another reason you need an elevator speech.

Please see attachment B for some examples of actual elevator speeches used by some of my clients. Notice that an elevator speech can be used by a twenty-year-old college student looking for summer work, as well as by a seasoned executive with thirty years' experience. Notice also that it works in all arenas—engineering, arts, finance, automotive repair, nursing, and marketing—any endeavor.

How do you build an elevator speech? You begin by listing your attributes. These are one-word labels that describe you. There are no right or wrong attributes. Sociable is just as valuable as shy. Followers are always needed, not just leaders. Detail-minded people are just as important as those with the big picture in mind. The most important aspect of this list is that each attribute be true about you.

If you have trouble identifying your attributes, then work with someone you trust or with a professional career coach and develop a list of questions that will help you decide those attributes that you think make you successful at what you do. You can ask your trusted advisor to help with this list or ask your significant other or any person that you believe will give you an unvarnished answer.

Take a look at the long list of attributes in the appendix. Circle as many as apply to you.

Jot down all the attributes that come to mind on the list in attachment A, bottom right hand corner of the page. Test them with people you trust. Then choose the top 5 that describe you. Rank order them from first to fifth. You may have circled twelve or fifteen of them or twenty-seven or thirty-two, but now you have to make some choices. The objective is to narrow them down to those attributes that (a) are true about you and (b) may interest an employer.

For example, you may say punctual, productive, mature, all of which are interesting to a hiring manager. You could also be romantic or spiritual, but an employer is probably not interested in those.

If you have narrowed down the list to about five, then it's time to construct a sentence that describes who you are, professionally. Take a look at some examples in attachment B.

The elevator speech is like a run-on sentence containing a number of key words that the interviewer can use to start or continue a conversation about you (more on how to use the elevator speech in CC-103—Interviews). Some of the key words you will use in your elevator speech are attributes; others are skills or experience. For example career wise you probably want to be known as a "commodity purchasing professional" or "corporate counsel" or "digital products price analyst" or "Internet security director" or whatever your current occupational circumstances. The skills, knowledge, and attributes that you pack around your elevator speech will lend substance and credibility.

Try your hand and draft an elevator speech. Begin by jotting down some attributes. Then try to build a sentence around them. Some people have a lot of difficulty with this. I often hear from clients that it is for them the hardest part of this preparation process. They say, "I don't know what to say about myself."

Begin with a simple draft, a short sentence about yourself. Then explain the process to someone you trust and try it out on a number of people. Ask them, after they heard your elevator speech, what words they remember. What attributes or skills would they want to pursue in conversation with you if they were a hiring manager?

If you make it too long, you'll have trouble remembering it, so break it up into two or three parts. Start with (a) who you are, (b) what you've done/where you've been (very briefly!), and (c) what you are looking for. If you break it up into a few parts, then that will help you remember it, as in "Okay, I have three parts to remember—who I am, where I've been, and what I want." That's it!

The Objective

Many candidates are taught by well-meaning coaches that they should begin their resume with their objective statement. Typically, the objective on their resumes reads, "Seeking challenging position where I can use my education, skills, and experience for growth and opportunity in a dynamic organization."

What's wrong with that? Seems reasonable. Unfortunately, it fails on many fronts.

First, it reads just like everyone else's objective. Second, it only says what the candidate wants (which presumes that the hiring manager is charitably interested). Third, the reader has just read the first paragraph but still doesn't know anything about the candidate. So frankly, it's a perfectly useless statement when redacted that way.

By contrast, if you use an elevator speech, then the reader is informed about *what the candidate has to offer*, which is distinguishably different from that of others. Placing your elevator speech at the top of the resume gives you, the candidate, a "face." The elevator speech begins to sketch out what kind of person you are.

The rest of the resume will be packed with information about your education, experience, skills, duties, and accomplishments; but it's the elevator speech in combination with your cover letter that defines you as a person for the reader. And in the end, gentle reader, when you are a finalist among two or three, it's *who you are* that will make the difference.

The Resume

The purpose of a resume is to get a job, right?
No.
The purpose of a resume is to get the first interview.

Employers use resumes for a number of reasons. An obvious one is to learn about your skills, knowledge, and attributes as outlined in the resume. This is a screening activity, where the recruiter or hiring manager basically separates or rank orders the candidates from apparent best to nonqualified. If the resume is of interest to the employer, s/he will use it to generate some questions for your interview. The resume is also the first glimpse the employer will have of your abilities to write (grammar, spelling, syntax, consistency, brevity, clarity, etc.). You must pay attention to detail, organize your thoughts, categorize your information, and communicate your message.

Let's revisit the story of Tara Whitman, mentioned in chapter 1. First, we discussed what she loves to do—project management, contract administration, customer relationship management, process optimization, office operations, administrative logistics, research and problem solving. Notice that she did not mention, when building the list of what she loves to do, anything about love for payables or a passion for receivables, databases, or ledgers. Tara and I then discussed how to build her resume so that her attributes would be demonstrated in the results and accomplishments of her work experience.

Competent Resumes versus Passionate Correspondence

Many resumes that cross my desk are poorly thought out, not well organized, inconsistent in style and format.

The better resumes are what I call "competent"—that is, they are fairly well designed, consistent in style and format, and they do a fairly good job of describing where the applicant has worked, their duties and responsibilities, the scope and reach of their charter as well as listing some of their accomplishments.

The problem is that even the competent resumes are lacking information about *how well* the applicant has done their job. So even the competent resumes read like a very long job description.

When discussing this problem of how well they've done their job with some of my clients, they often reply,

> *Well, I'll tell them how well I performed in those jobs when I'm in the interview.*

Can you picture in your mind my wry smile? My response is,

> *And why do you believe you'll get an interview, given that your resume reads like a two-page job description, and you have not even once demonstrated with facts or figures how well you did your job? How is the reader to know that you are more effective and efficient than the person you would replace?*

Don't Drive in the Rearview Mirror

If you could see me while racing my sports car doing one lap of the track, and you watched my eyes, how much time would I spend looking at the rearview mirror? Typically, I look at the rearview mirror as I approach a curve on the track, looking to see if anyone is coming up from behind to outbrake me into that corner, or going down the fast straights, casually looking up at the mirror to see if anyone is gaining on me. Basically, I look in the rearview mirror for safety. But I spend very little time there. The vast majority of the time I'm looking at the road ahead, to where I want to be, not where I've been.

Your resume reeks of where you've been!
—Hannah Morgan, career coach

Your resume must point to where you want to go. Not just in the objective at the top, but through the body of the resume, the reader must have a sense that you know what you're good at, and you know what you want. For example if you've been a finance executive with a multitude of responsibilities, but what you love is the operational aspects of running the enterprise, then your resume should have a lot of content that speaks to what you want. This means that if you've been working for twenty plus years, you will not be able to include everything you've ever done. You'll have to make hard choices and discard those things that you'd rather not be doing in the future, no matter how much or how well you did them in the past, and make room to discuss those experiences and skills that you want to continue to use in your next assignment.

Answering the "So what?" Question

Once you've organized your chronological resume into a competent resume, the easiest part is done.

The difficult part, as many of my clients tell me, is answering the "So what?" question. This means thinking about those things you've done very well, and then specifically demonstrating how well you did it. For example, if you write, "Responsible for sales of building supplies in New York, New Jersey, and Connecticut."

So what? All that tells the reader is that the applicant was responsible for selling office building hardware in a three-state area. But how well did s/he do it?

Here's how to answer the "So what?" question:

"Responsible for book of business in New York, New Jersey, and Connecticut:

- Exceeded sales quota by 21% over previous year.
- Reduced customer complaints by 43%.
- Improved sales to delivery times by 12%.
- Received several memos from management praising my performance.
- Finished the year at third highest among seventeen representatives."

Some would argue that I picked an easy example, a sales career, where everything is easily measured. And that's true. The sad fact is that some sales professionals fail to point out their own metrics on their resumes. But to show how it can be done, please take a look at the sample resume that I've included in attachment D. That resume belongs to a friend, a training professional. The resume content is intact except that her name and company names have been disguised.

The problem you face when building a resume is to look objectively at the work you're doing and measure it quantitatively and qualitatively to demonstrate how well you've done it.

Whether your career choice is easily quantifiable and readily yields metrics—or not—you still have to find ways to measure and quantify *the value of your contribution*. This can be done in any career.

If you cannot measure the value of what you do, then you can rest assured that you are not the only one who notices. Your manager and your peers and subordinates will know that what you're doing can either be done better by someone else or discarded or outsourced. So measure your value you must!

Measuring the Value of Your Contribution

One of my clients, Beverlie, was a professional harp player, piano player, and teacher. Beverlie had been sending out her resume to many school districts but was not getting any responses. Upon reading her resume, everyone agreed it was a competent resume. The problem was that the school districts were receiving many resumes as good as hers. There was little in her resume that distinguished it from those of many others. I asked her,

Beverlie, are you a good music teacher?

Oh yes, of course I am.

Okay, but from reading your resume, how do I know that you're really good?

Beverlie lit up like a Christmas tree:

Well, you should see what the parents say, what the students say about me. I get letters, commendations. I get many compliments for playing my harp at weddings. I've been told by some students and parents that I'm the best music teacher they've ever had!

Beverlie's eyes were now as big as saucers as she related her achievements to me. Her face demonstrated the passion that she had for playing the harp and for teaching music. I had no doubt that she is as good as she said she was. The challenge for her was to demonstrate in her resume and cover letter that she was far above average, that she was an *excellent,* an *extraordinary* piano and harp teacher.

> *Beverlie, you've convinced me that you are really passionate about playing the harp and teaching music. But I don't see that in your cover letter or in your resume.*
>
> *Oh, but you can't say things like that in a cover letter or on a resume.*
>
> *Why not?*
>
> *Well, you just don't. It's not professional.*

The Cover Letter

Beverlie was functioning under the assumption that demonstrating one's passion and love for one's chosen career was not really professional. If she would do it at all, she related, she would only do it during an interview, face-to-face. However, even then she confessed she would have been guarded, reticent, careful with her words—in other words, professional.

Where is your passion? If you are going to spend a significant portion of your week—indeed, of your life—in some work activities, wouldn't you want those activities to at least have some measure of love or passion in your life? I hope your answer would be "yes" to that question. How do you convey your love, your passion, for certain work activities?

You do so via the cover letter.

The cover letter is brief and to the point. It's only one page. And it only has three paragraphs. The three paragraphs are as follows:

a. Use an emotional hook in your first paragraph.
b. Include the words *love* and *passion* in your second paragraph.
c. Mention three to five attributes in your third and last paragraph with a note that you'll be calling to follow up.

The Emotional Hook

The best way to start a cover letter is to be able to say, in the first sentence of your first paragraph, something along these lines:

> "I was referred to your office by (name of someone known to the person to whom you're writing)."

Or,

> "We have a friend in common—(person's name) tells me that he is part of your organization."

Or,

> "I was in temple last Friday, and I learned that (person's name) sees you regularly at your daughter's soccer games."

This approach sets what I call "the emotional hook." The recipient knows immediately that there is a second-degree connection between the two of you. This is the best way to establish a personal connection, only two degrees apart from your target audience. This reassures her/him because it provides a built-in reference source *even before they've read your resume*!

Since this is the preferred approach, using a second-degree connection, then the best way, indeed the only way, for you to build a vast database of second-degree connections is to *go out and begin networking*.

Conversely, the worst approach begins this way: "I am responding to your Help Wanted advertisement."

If this approach is the only one available, then by all means use it. But the best approach is to establish a second-degree connection in the first sentence of your letter. And to do that, you must begin your networking. More specifics about strategies and tactics for networking are found later in this chapter.

The *Love* Word and the *Passion* Word

You might think, *Wait, isn't that kind of corny and not really "professional," using those words* love *and* passion *in work-related correspondence?*

Clients like Beverlie are very hesitant to use these words in their job search correspondence. They tell me that they've never seen that before, that it would not look professional. I understand their hesitancy, but there is more than one approach.

The straightforward approach is simply to say something like:

> "While I was at KPMG, I loved meeting new clients and learning their requirements."

Or,

> "Throughout my seven years with Kraft, I demonstrated my passion for manufacturing production quality."

Surely that wasn't so hard. Actually, maybe you didn't even notice that I used the *love* word and the *passion* word.

But there is another way, besides using first person singular. That's the convenience of third-person singular, as in this example:

> "My manager wrote in my performance appraisal that my love for statistical analysis is demonstrable."

Or,

> "Several customers attested to my passion for following up to ensure complete customer satisfaction."

In these examples the *love* and *passion* words are used to describe the writer—you—so they are objective in their source and just as powerful.

The Third and Last Paragraph

To close your brief cover letter you should now give them a little insight into your personal self by appropriately mentioning three of your top attributes, as in, "Perhaps your enterprise can take advantage of my dedication to GAAP in payroll practices, my integrity, and my tenacity in forensics to improve the operations of your payroll department. I will call your office to follow up on [name the date]."

Always finish with a note that you will be following up, and then jot it in your calendar so that you close the loop with them.

The Next Best Thing

While you're on the hunt, always, *always* have a plan B!

- Sit down and explore the next best thing in case your ideal plan fails to work.
- Even if you are a finalist for three positions—keep looking!

Here's why. In November 1995, just before Thanksgiving, I was a finalist for three positions, all of them as vice president of human resources. My wife and I went to see my career counselor, Ted, to brief him on my progress. I pointed out to Ted that things were looking good—I was a finalist for three positions.

Ted said,

Have you thought about what you will do if you don't get any of them?

What do you mean, Ted? I'm a finalist for three big jobs, two in the Washington area and one in New Jersey.

Yes, but what if you don't get any of them?

Ted, I'm sure I'll get one of them. Probably two. Maybe a clean sweep! Wouldn't that be sweet!

Yes, that would be sweet. But what's your plan if you don't get any of them?

I didn't have a plan B.

And I didn't get any of the three jobs.

What followed from that point was months of frustration and agony. It was November, so everyone turned their attention to their Thanksgiving holiday plans followed by Christmas and New Year's.

During those six to eight weeks, recruiting activities will slow down or stop in many companies. Many organizations have fiscal years ending on December 31. A typical comment around that time is, "Well, we have to finish with a strong bottom line this year, so we're not doing any hiring until next year. We can't even hire replacements for those who have left."

What can be learned from this experience?

Always, always keep looking!

Don't stop interviewing, calling, networking, reaching out to people and sending out correspondence even while you are a finalist for a position.

You must maintain the momentum!

In a job search, the gestation period for a good-paying job can be very long, and losing just a few days can set the gestation process back, especially just before holidays.

Always keep looking, keep filling that pipeline with meetings and networking connections, and another interview or two.

Chapter Summary

In this second chapter, you have been provided an outline for construction of essential tools for your job search. Explicit directions have been provided for you so you can build:

- An elevator speech, which describes your skills, experience, and attributes quickly and effectively;
- Your professional objective, stated crisply, with clarity;
- A passionate resume, which depicts those professional activities and personal interests for which you have a passion, and one that answers the "So what?" question; and
- A brief but effective cover letter.

This chapter also emphasized the importance of measuring your value added, measuring your professional contribution. The effectiveness of using the emotional hook was emphasized as an opening sentence in the cover letter to immediately connect with the reader. The importance of using the *love* word and *passion* word was explained with examples. In the instructions for the cover letter, the importance of the third paragraph was explained, wherein you should ask for assistance in expanding your network and indicating that you will be following up.

One crucial tenet of this chapter is the concept that you should always, always keep looking for the next best thing. The critical value of networking was emphasized and examples provided.

Homework

1. Draft an elevator speech using the top 5 attributes that you think best describe you, and include it in your resume as you make changes. Refer to sample elevator speeches in attachment B.
2. Take a look at the elevator speech that you drafted—make sure your elevator speech uses the top 5 attributes that you think best describe you. Include this elevator speech at the top of your resume.
3. Go through each accomplishment in your resume and make sure that you answer the "So what?" question at the end of each achievement using facts and figures or even testimonials whenever possible. See sample resume of June Farnsworth, attachment D. Examples:

   - "Increased efficiency of manufacturing process yielding 17% less defective products and saving $172,000."

- "Responsible for helping customers try on their dresses and outfits in junior department of Macy's. Received four letters of commendation from retail customers."
- "Accountable for problem solving in the field, diagnosing electrical faults and service interruption. Commended by supervisor for efficient, courteous service."
- "Helped attorneys draft their briefs by researching our legal database, enabling them to spend more time strategizing their approach to litigation."
- "Improved sales closure rate from 34% to 46% year over year, helping the top line by $3.1 million."
- "Reduced time to market of new consumer electronics from average 10 months to just over 7 months."

2. Draft a cover letter using the template in attachment C. Pretend you are writing to a target company or hiring manager. Write as if you actually wanted an interview opportunity. Make sure you use an emotional hook in your first paragraph, include the words *love* and *passion* in your second paragraph, and mention three to five attributes in your third and last paragraph.
3. Choose an environment where you think you might want to work. You can research environments using *The Book of Lists* published by business journals in most cities. Make a brief list of those environments where you think you'd like to work and also another list of those places where you know you would *not* like to work.
4. Use an Internet Web browser (Yahoo, Google) to search for networking groups. Join at least two groups and *start going to their meetings*.
5. Use these attachments found in the back of the book: cold networking call (attachment F) and warm networking call (attachment G) as necessary tools to conduct your networking calls.

> *I just landed a job following the suggestions I found in* Getting There.
> *I liked the concrete, easy-to-understand-and-execute approach. I also found it helped me deal with some serious problems that were holding me back. The book helped me to remember the kinds of things I used to love to do, and now I'm headed in the right direction.*
> *This book is a great investment.*
> —Jim Striegel, senior software engineer

THREE

CAREER COACHING 103

The Interview

Interviews

The purpose of the first interview is to get the job, right?
No.
The purpose of the first interview is to get the second interview.
Don't worry about hitting a home run, just hit a single!
Here's what I mean. I used to coach my daughter and her fast-pitch softball team. Alison is not a big girl, and we knew that she had a slim chance or none of hitting the ball hard to the outfield. Alison's strength was that she was a fast runner. She was so quick her nickname was Scooter. So the plan was to get her to first base.

Alison, just bunt or take four balls or even get hit by the pitch! Just get to first base, and you can steal from there.

Sure enough, she would typically bunt or take a walk to first.
With Alison standing on first, I would signal to her: "Go on the first pitch." Everyone knew that Alison would steal second base on the first pitch. She did this for years. There were very few catchers who could catch the pitch, stand up, and throw over the pitcher to second before Alison reached the bag. After stealing second, she would steal third, and eventually advance to home plate.

So using the analogy above, the idea is to focus on the upcoming interview. Prepare thoroughly for it. The objective is to do very well at this point (first base), and thereby increase the chances of advancing to the next interview (second base).

If you've done your homework at the end of CC-101 and CC-102, you are now ready to take interviews. There is no need to stress yourself. If you do all the work to prepare appropriately, the chances are pretty good that you will be better organized than the person interviewing you.

What follows is an interviewing strategy, plus some tips and tactics.

Three Tools for the Interview

If you follow the process suggested below, you will be armed with three things that you need for a successful interview.

One: You will have an answer to their first question, which is likely to be, "Tell me about yourself," or "What have you been doing (professionally)?" or even "Why are you here?" Whatever the form of their question, you will be prepared, and they will be impressed with your prompt and concise reply.

Two: You will have a list of *all that they want* from a candidate. They will be impressed with your *anticipation of their concerns* and with the quality of your answers *to their problems*. Notice that I didn't say your objectives. They couldn't care any less about your career objectives. That's not why you're there. *Focus on them.* You're there to solve *their problem*, not yours.

Three: You will know what questions to ask of them and in what order, so they will be impressed with your analytical skills and sense of process discipline.

To help you with the first interview, these are the questions that you will be asked; following those some that you will ask.

One: The First Question That You Will Be Asked

Let's now work on the first question that a recruiter or hiring manager is likely to ask you. The question "Tell me about yourself" can be used by the recruiter or hiring manager as the warm-up question, or after a chat about the weather or your travel experience while getting to the interview.

This question, *no matter what form it takes*, will be asked in the early part of the interview process.

It can take the form of "What adjectives would others use to describe you?" You would use your top 5 attributes that are part of your elevator speech to answer that question.

Another variant could be "What interests you about this job that we posted?" You would tailor your elevator speech, on the fly, toward the position for which you are interviewing. The objective is to hijack the question, in a very nice subtle way, and answer it in such a way that you effectively set the agenda, describing your skills, knowledge, and attributes.

Yet another form it could take could be, "I see you have a strong manufacturing background, but how will that help you in our finance and banking organization?" Your elevator speech will have anticipated this potential pushback from the hiring manager, and it would contain key words that will serve to calm their fears.

For example, if they ask, "Why are you interested in this company, ITX?" you may respond with your elevator speech nested in a natural response, such as,

> *My good friend, Melissa, who works in your marketing department, alerted me that ITX was interested in expanding their online and social media marketing team. I am a results-driven, experienced marketing manager with eleven years in the business-to-business space, employing my compassionate but firm people management skills to lead teams in accomplishing extraordinary things.*

At this point, it's important to pause, let the words sink in, and let the recruiter or hiring manager choose what to ask you about—your team leadership, your compassion, or your B to B marketing technical experience. Even at this early stage of the interview, at the first sentence of the conversation, you've already laid out an agenda—on your terms.

For any variant of this question, when asked early in the interview exchange, you will always have a crisp answer—your elevator speech. This is the same elevator speech that you designed and wrote in CC-102, which you wrote at the top of your resume.

Keep in mind you have to answer the question using the *content* of your elevator speech, sounding natural and smooth in your delivery. You can't be stiff or awkward in your delivery. I actually had to use my elevator speech at a neighborhood picnic standing near the swimming pool wearing shorts and sandals while holding a beer. That's not the time to be formal, but I still got the message out.

Practice using your elevator speech with a trusted advisor. Let them ask you the first question in various forms and learn different ways to answer it while delivering the *content* of the answer. It's critical that the interviewer hear the key words that you are trying to convey—the substance of your message.

Behavioral Interviewing

Some people have heard of behavioral interviewing techniques, and they profess being afraid of them. I frankly don't understand why. The purpose of a behavioral interview question, when properly presented, is to learn how the candidate handled or managed a situation in the past.

A behavioral interview question does not have the word *would* in it, as in "What would you do if . . ." such and such a situation were to arise. The behavioral interview question always looks to the past and asks what you *did* under such and such circumstances. The rationale for asking it this way is that social research shows that people are likely to respond the same way in the future as they have in the past, when similar circumstances are present.

A behavioral interview should be very easy for anyone to answer. The key to the response, indeed, the key to all healthy relationships, is to tell the truth, the unvarnished truth. The employer who properly uses behavioral-based interviewing is trying to assess if you fit into the organizational culture and your ability to succeed in the new position.

Here is a sample of some behavioral interview questions and what to do in preparing your response:

- "Have you been in a situation when you inherited a team of people who were totally demoralized by their previous management? What did you do about it?"
- "The last time that you started a new job, what did you do in the first few days?"
- "Tell me about a time when you saw a colleague cheat on her expense account. What did you do?"
- "Can you tell me about a time when you embarked on a project that turned into a failure? What was it about, and how did you handle it?"
- "Tell us about a time when you had to convince others of your point of view."
- "Have you ever had a manager who was very difficult to work with? Tell me about the circumstances (no names) and how you handled it."

There may be some behavioral interviewing questions that don't link directly to anything in your work history. For example, maybe you've never seen anyone cheating on their expense account, or maybe you have never managed a group of people. In those instances, you can *use your attributes to reply*, saying what you would do. So you could reply saying, "I'm very *respectful* of other people's talents, skills, and integrity; so if I inherited a disillusioned team, I would trust and engage them in such a way that they could each shine in their own area of skill and expertise."

Or you may have a related experience, such as observing someone doing something wrong, and modify your answer to the question accordingly. For example, "I've never observed someone cheating on their expense report, but I did find a candidate who lied about his college degree. After confirming with the college that our candidate did not graduate, and asking him to explain the discrepancy (during which time he agreed that he had falsely reported his degree), I conferred with the hiring manager. Based on the company's core value of "integrity," we decided to walk away from the candidate who was otherwise highly qualified."

Handling Other Questions That May Arise

This book will not attempt to anticipate every question that an employer may ask. In fact, there are many specialized books dealing with the questions that may arise accompanied by suggestions for responses. Employers may ask questions from any number of perspectives. Here is a sampling of the types of inquiries that some hiring managers may want to employ:

- What are your strengths? What are your weaknesses?
- If I asked some people who know you well to describe you, what three words would they use?
- What did you love about your most recent position? What did you dislike doing?
- What are your career goals for the next three, five, ten years?
- Why do you want to work in our organization?
- How will you achieve your professional objectives in our organization?
- Have you read about our new market segmentation strategy? What do you think of it?
- What can your next manager do in order to help your career?
- In what ways do you think you can make a contribution to our organization?
- What is our reputation in the community? What are people saying about our company?
- Why did you choose that course of study?
- Were you ever fired from or asked to leave a job? What happened?
- What extracurricular activities have you been involved in? Why those?
- Where do you see yourself in five years?

This last question is not a particularly valuable question, in my view, because nowadays there are positions and even whole industries that did not even exist five years earlier. The question may be suited for traditional, mature industries with very well established structures—finance, manufacturing, not-for-profit management. But this type of question must be handled differently if your work environment is information technology, Internet multilevel marketing, or computer gaming. Regardless of the relevancy of the question, however, you'll be more confident if you're prepared to answer whatever questions you might encounter.

There are whole books devoted to interviewing questions, so we won't try to cover them all in this publication. But, certainly, if you want to ensure that you have thought about many forms of questions that a recruiter may throw at you, or that you could pose to them, I would refer you to many publications and even Web sites, which would be very helpful.

Some Questions You Hope They Don't Ask

Some hiring managers want to play with the candidate, consciously or unconsciously, or to show off or needle the candidate to see a reaction. These questions have no rational purpose, but some insist on asking them, and they are quite proud of how clever they are. Here are some examples:

- I have very high expectations of you in this interview. Are you going to disappoint me?
- How soon after you start will you want my job?
- Do you like the Yankees or the Red Sox? Be careful, your answer may seal your destiny!
- If you were told to bunny hop down the hall, would you do it? Why? Why not? (I have actually been asked this question!)
- Would you rather be a monkey or a zebra, and why?

Yes, gentle reader, those questions, and others that are not fit to print, have actually been asked.

Illegal Questions That Employers Should Never Ask

Let's set the record straight. It is the responsibility of every hiring manager to discriminate.

That's right. Every hiring manager discriminates. They must.

That's the whole purpose of the interview—to discriminate among all the candidates on the basis of legal factors: education, experience, credentials, attributes, and the like.

Employers are *prohibited* from discriminating on the basis of factors deemed illegal, such as race, religion, sex, nationality, marital status, age, physical ability/disability, etc.

The following questions would constitute a violation of federal or state laws concerning terms and conditions of employment if they were asked anytime, from preemployment through employment and even postemployment:

- How old are you?
- What's your nationality?
- Where were your parents born?
- What is your birth date?
- With whom do you live?
- Are you married, divorced, single?
- Are you disabled?
- How many children do you have?
- Who is going to take care of your children while you are at work?
- How much do you weigh?
- When was your last physical exam?
- Have you ever been arrested?

Note: Some of these questions, i.e., "What is your birth date?" and "What is your marital status?" are legal and necessary to ask after the job offer has been made and accepted for purposes of health and life insurance and/or tax withholding documentation.

How do you respond to those illegal questions? The fact is that you can go ahead and answer any of them. It's up to you. You do have a few alternatives:

- You can answer the question about where your parents were born, for example, and emphasize that as a result of their many work-related relocations, you have learned to become very adaptable.
- Or you can decline to provide an answer, but doing it in such a way that it doesn't break the relationship you are trying to establish (if indeed it's worth establishing—one thing is to ask an illegal question out of ignorance of regulations; another is having intent to discriminate, but you have to decide this on the spot).
- Or you might want to examine the rationale behind the question, such as if they ask about citizenship because of requirements for a Department of Defense contractor.

Some Exceptions

In some circumstances, employers have a responsibility to ensure that certain parameters are met, such as employment contingent on passing a drug test, background check (evaluation of conviction records that pertain to the job in question), US citizenship for national security clearance, gender in the case of male model/female model for merchandising, etc. However, in those instances the employer bears the responsibility and burden that the preemployment requirements are directly tied to the job opportunity.

Two: The T-Chart
Their Needs and Your Contributions

The second way to prepare for the interview is to write your T-chart for interviewing. You simply take a piece of paper, write a line down the middle of it, top to bottom, then a line across the top, about one inch from the top of the page (see attachment E). Then on the top left you write, "What they want" and on the right, "What I can offer or contribute."

Now the real work begins—to understand what they want and concisely write it down as bullets on the left side of the page. You can get this information from their job descriptions and the notes you took during a phone interview. It's also very helpful if you can gather information from insiders. That's where LinkedIn is so important, to learn from others what's going on inside (more about LinkedIn in chapter 9).

If you're using your personal computer to do this, write everything you know about the position on the left side of your T-chart. Identify those desired items in a list as bullets, in any order. Then go back and prioritize them based on what you know about the company, its mission, your hiring manager's priorities, and any other data points you have.

The objective is to build a roster of all their needs, their problems, their desired skills and experience in an orderly, prioritized list.

Now that you know what they want, bullet by bullet, it's time to write down how you would help them with each of their problems. Remember, you are the answer to their business problem.

Think about your experience. For each of their requirements (on the left of the T-chart), write down on the right side of the T-chart something you've done, something you have accomplished that fulfills that requirement. It's important here that you are crisp but complete, so that when the item comes up you can readily respond to it with clarity and conciseness.

Actually, to optimize this technique, you should give the T-chart to a trusted advisor so they can quiz you. You should spend about a half hour rehearsing questions and answers. This will quickly build confidence between their potential questions and your answers. By practicing your answers, they will be right on the tip of your tongue for quick and complete response.

If there is a gap in your knowledge or skills, write down one or two attributes that would help you achieve that level or expertise. For example, you could say, "While my strength is in compensation, not benefits, I am a *collaborative* person who *works well cross-functionally* in a *participative style*, so I will seek out the advice and counsel of your resident experts in the benefits area."

Three: The Questions That You Must Ask

These are the three questions you will ask the recruiter, beginning with a large overarching blue sky topic and moving to smaller more immediate topics in the order found below:

- **One:** "What can you tell me about this company, its culture, its founder, its recent event that I read about in the news?"

  - o Prepare to ask this question by visiting the Web site, understanding a brief history of the company, learning about its founder or current CEO.
  - o Try to find recent news events, which are often found in their Web site.
  - o Be cognizant of the company's products and services, recent acquisitions, thrusts in new market directions, major competitors, and research breakthroughs. Also, learn about the company's industry and its trends for growth, threats, and opportunities.
  - o Study the company's reach and scope—is it local, regional, national, multinational, or global?
  - o Learn about the company's values and organizational culture by reading about them in their Web site or in trade and business magazines.
  - o Use LinkedIn to identify some people who work at that company, to learn about its ways and its corporate culture.
  - o Then, armed with information about the company, ask some broad, overarching blue sky questions.

- **Two:** "Would you please describe to me the division, group, subsidiary, facility that I'll be working in?"

  - o At this point, you may ask about the team or division that you might be working in—its mission, its location, its operating principles.

o Try to determine the degree of autonomy of this group or division from the parent or corporate entity.

- **Three:** "Would you please provide me some insight about the team, hiring manager, and peers that I'll be working with?"

    o Now that you have carefully and logically approached the subject, you can ask questions about the person you'll be reporting to (you may not yet know them, if you are on your first telephone or personal interview).
    o You can ask about your peers, their styles of work, and their day-to-day practices.

Why is it important to ask the above questions in the order suggested? Because human nature being what it is, if you start in the opposite order, you'll soon digress into smaller and smaller details and never have the opportunity to ask questions in levels 1 and 2. By asking questions in this order, top to bottom, it causes you to research the whole company and shows that you are interested in the whole enterprise and your potential effectiveness within it, not just in your parochial personal job concerns.

Preparing for the Second Interview

How do you stand out like mad during your second interview?
How do I differentiate myself from other more experienced candidates?
Do I bring a pizza or ride in on a unicycle?
—Alison Martínez, from one of her e-mails

The answer to this depends on the signals they gave you on the first interview.

What problems did they say need to be addressed? If you picked up on the problems that they are currently experiencing, then you need to demonstrate that you can address them with your skills, knowledge, and attributes. This way you're ahead of the person who was not paying attention.

All employers have problems that need solving, or they have plans that they want to execute. Even if the former incumbent was very good in his or her job, there are always ways for you to improve the situation. The point is this—identify their problem (if you're not sure what it is, then just ask! *You will get points for wanting to know.*) After you learn about their problem, then propose a solution, or at least a vision of how to make improvements—ways to make things better. Make sure you ask all the pertinent questions about this—thereby sending a signal that you are interested in their problems, their agenda, and their future.

Second and third interviews are often very much like the first but with different people. They can be quite boring to an experienced candidate with a history of many interviews. Use the same process, that is, begin asking your questions at the highest level, continuing through the division level down through to the position you desire.

Tips and Tactics for Interviewing

It goes without saying that you have to research the company with whom you are interviewing. So why do I go on and state the obvious? Because some people fail to do it. The Internet has made researching any company, or any topic, very easy. No need to look for news items about your target company through dusty periodicals in the public library. It's easy to research your target company; it leaves you no excuse for not having done it.

Make sure you understand the history of the company. This is particularly true for companies founded by individuals who have achieved iconic status like Microsoft (Bill Gates), Apple (Steve Jobs), Dell (Michael Dell), FedEx (Freddie Smith).

This notion also holds true in regional markets. If you live in a community like Rochester, New York, it would be inexcusable if you applied for a position at Paychex and had not heard of its founder (Tom Golisano) or at Constellation Brands (Robert and Richard Sands) or Wegmans Food Markets (Robert Wegman, now deceased) or PAETEC (Arunas Chesonis).

Do's and Don'ts for Interviewing

Do: dress appropriately for the interview. This is where inside information is very helpful. Some companies allow wide amplitude in business wear and rarely insist on white shirt and ties. But others stick to what they think will work best with their clients. One very successful company in Rochester is noted for its dress code and conduct—including entry doors reserved for the customers and visitors, another door for managers, and another one for the balance of employees.

Don't: sit in front of the person interviewing you in a perfectly symmetrical position. If you are sitting in a chair with arms, lean slightly to one side or the other. In other words, the left side of your body should look different than the right side. Why is this important? It denotes that you're comfortable, confident, and able to handle this situation without being overly stiff or rigid.

At one time my employer sent me to California to investigate a race discrimination case. One of the persons that I had to interview was a vice president of the division. She was a minority female, and when she came to meet with me, she was clearly apprehensive and skeptical. She didn't like having to participate in this sort of thing. I sensed that, and I knew I had to defuse the situation to obtain her cooperation. As we sat down, the lady sat across the table from me, symmetrically, with her hands folded in front of her on top of the table. She appeared tense. I adopted a very relaxed sitting posture. Leaning back in the armchair, I crossed my left leg over my right and used a notepad on my lap to write down her responses. My tone of voice was relaxed, my demeanor conveyed that I had done this many times, and I knew what had to be done, efficiently. After some dialogue over several minutes, I saw that she also leaned back in her chair, eventually crossed one leg over the other, and started swinging her high heel shoe from the tip of her toes. I knew then that she was onboard. I set the tone with my voice and body language. She cooperated in her role, and the investigation was successfully concluded.

Do: be punctual. If you've never been to the location of the interview, give yourself extra time: what if there is an accident on the expressway? What if you can't find the building in a large industrial complex?

Don't: fly in on the morning of the interview—so many things can go awry. For interviews that require long distance travel, arriving the night before greatly improves the chances of being on time. Many airlines are booked solid and bump you off, and sometimes flights are canceled due to weather, maintenance problems and lack of airplanes.

Do: give a firm handshake. Look the person in the eye as you shake hands. If necessary, repeat their name to make sure you have it. It will help you get it right and remember it. Better to repeat it now, during introductions, rather than forget what it was and be embarrassed later.

Don't: volunteer negative information. Be truthful about the question being asked, but don't add negative content that wasn't asked for. For example, if the hiring manager asks, "Why did you leave that job?" You can tell her, "Because they wanted someone with more marketing experience, and I decided I'd rather concentrate on Web services." You should not say, "Because my manager was a self-centered, controlling, detail-obsessed, micromanager with delusions of grandeur who would not even consider any other opinion."

Do: be polite and very courteous to the clerical or support staff that you meet at the interview location. That should go without saying, but it's often overlooked, and it can be part of the deciding factors. Here is an example of what can be done. As I was drafting this book, I had occasion to interview in a Fortune 500 company. There were six interviews scheduled for that day; and one person, a recruiting coordinator named Idris, had made all the arrangements, which I know is a lot of painstaking detailed work. After the interviews, I sent the customary personalized thank-you letters to each of my interviewers. But I also sent one to Idris even though I had not met her. She replied within minutes by e-mail—she was so excited to receive her own thank-you letter! It's obvious this had not happened to her before.

This reminds me of another story. When I was in high school, I attended a party at a beautiful apartment in New York City. After being there for a while, I went downstairs, outside, to get some fresh air. I then struck up a conversation with an older fellow, also standing outside. He said he worked in the TV and movie industry as a grip. I remarked that it must be exciting to meet and work among television and movie stars. He said, "Yes, it is," and that he always told them one thing: "Be nice to me on your way up because I'm still going to be here on your way down." I have never forgotten that advice.

Don't: look away or down at your feet when your host is talking to you. Look them in the eye and respond with nods or shaking of the head as appropriate to let her/him know you've understood.

Do: listen to the entire question before answering it. This becomes particularly hard to do as you become a more experienced candidate and after many interviews. It's important to discipline yourself to wait until the entire question has been asked.

Don't: chew gum or candy or fidget or ramble or slouch (see above for body language).

Do: allow the hiring managers to do most of the talking, if they are so inclined. Many hiring managers will spend forty-five out of sixty minutes describing the job, the company, the management, the joys of golf in Pebble Beach, whatever. Then, at the end they'll say, "I've had the most enjoyable interview with you!" Take it in stride. That person will go and tell all the others what a wonderful (listener) candidate you are. And it's true.

Don't: discuss your salary expectations too early in the game. If you've done your homework, particularly with your insider contacts, you should know that they will offer you something within 10 to 15 percent of your targeted salary. If your expectations are exceedingly high or if their pay practices are below the norm, you were not meant for each other.

Do: ask open questions that require the interviewer to reveal information. One tip given to me by a sales professional is that if the interviewer is not very cooperative, or seems to be holding back, you can say, "Oh?" in a voice tone as in, "Really?" or "Is that a fact?" It compels the interviewer to explain more.

Don't: ask closed questions that can be easily answered with a yes or a no.

Do: smile.

> *Papi, in the last half hour or so I did an internet search on second*
> *interviews and looked at about 10 websites. They don't even come close*
> *to the depth you have here in your book!*
> Alison Martínez, from one of her e-mails

My daughter, Alison, had been following my suggestion—always, always keep looking. She was a finalist for three fund-raising positions in the Rochester, New York, area. One hiring manager went as far as saying to her in her last interview, "You're definitely what we're looking for. Just let me discuss it with my manager. When can you start?" But within two days, she received three letters and phone calls informing her that she was not the chosen candidate. Just like that. She went from almost celebrating a new position that she was assured was hers to nothing. You can imagine how upset she was.

My wife and I sat down with Alison and listened to her description of the kinds of jobs she had interviewed for, the environments that she would have been working in, and the attributes of the people that she had met. It became apparent that there were gaps, sometimes even polar differences, in their attributes and how they each viewed the world, which may have made her tenure in any of these positions disagreeable or impossible. Now, that may sound like a sour grapes story, but there is also another side, that as one door (or three doors) close, other doors open. Alison kept on looking and applying for positions even as she knew she was a finalist. Within a few days, she was called back to interviews for a fund-raising position at her alma mater, the University of Rochester, to meet with the dean of academic affairs, the chief administrative officer, and the president of the university hospital. Incredible. Even I, the skeptic, began to believe that she was finally close to landing. But it was not to be. She received more rejection letters—from her alma mater!

Handling Rejection

> *Job search is 100 percent rejection, because as soon as you land a job, the*
> *search is over.*
> —Orville Pierson

It was, I must admit, a difficult time for Alison and for us. She had been unemployed for five months since coming back from the Galapagos Islands, where she had been volunteer English teacher. It was tough to keep up her spirits in spite of so many close calls without job offers. Her savings were dwindling, and she was depressed about the way she was treated by coworkers at a local coffee shop where she worked to raise some cash. The way Alison faced into it was by sticking with her overall strategy, which was—keep looking, keep networking, following up on every lead.

Alison finally landed at a prominent not-for-profit organization. She was named marketing and annual giving manager, a sizeable title and accompanying responsibilities for a young person. She attributes her success to being cognizant of self, putting her attributes up front, and doing all the necessary tasks. Since that time, with the experience and contacts that she gained, she launched her own consulting enterprise, advising small not-for-profits on how to raise money for their cause.

Your Sunshine Folder

In the course of your job search, you should create a sunshine folder. A sunshine folder is simply a manila folder, preferably bright yellow, where you put thank-you notes, well wishes, e-mails, and other mementos that have been given to you from time to time for things you've done for other people.

What? You don't have any thank-you notes to put in your folder? Well, one of two things is at play: You haven't helped anyone, or you've helped some people, but they haven't had the courtesy to thank you.

You may ask, what's all this have to do with handling rejection? A sunshine folder is a tool that I use when I'm feeling down, for any reason, but it's something that I developed to get me through those long winter months of unemployment.

The sunshine folder reminds you that there are people who do care, and because of that, there is hope.

How to Handle Exploratory Interviews

An exploratory interview is simply a conversation that you request with a manager in a target company. This form of interviewing is a tool that you can use to

1.   penetrate a target company,
2.   hone your interviewing skills,
3.   expand your network,

4. generate new leads,
5. announce to hiring managers that you are in a search, and
6. decide if *you* want to work in that organization.

The kinds of questions that are raised during an exploratory interview are just like the ones mentioned above. The only difference is that in an exploratory interview, you are not discussing a particular vacancy in the organization. Instead you are sensing your way around with your questions, trying to see what problems they have in their organization, and how your skills, experience, and attributes may be brought to bear on them. Likewise, the person(s) interviewing you is/are sensing how you may be able to help them.

Notice that I said that an exploratory interview is a conversation. That's how it should feel. It is not a presentation. It is not a lecture or a monologue of your skills and experience. It's more akin to meeting someone at your favorite watering hole and discussing your career with them. It should feel light, interesting, and even fun. It's critical that they see you as you are. If they don't like how you really are, you don't belong there, and this is the best and easiest way to find out.

The Purpose of This Interview Is—To Get the Next Interview!

During your preparation for and throughout your interview process, you must bear in mind your key objective, which is to be such a compelling candidate that they'll just have to call you back for the next round of interviews. To hope or believe that your first interview will result in a job offer is incompatible with all but the most inconsequential of jobs. If you are applying at the Dairy Queen, the franchise owner may offer you a position as a cashier at the end of the first interview. But if you want to manage opening and closing the store along with the second or third shift of DQ employees, she will probably want to think about it, check your references, and ask you back (you hope) for a second round.

What Are They Really Buying? Your Attributes!

This is particularly true in higher levels of operations management, strategy, or planning positions. An engineer may become a vice president of strategy; a CPA/MBA becomes a chief technology officer; a PhD in physical chemistry becomes a worldwide vice president general manager; a master's level electrical engineer becomes chief operating officer (those are just a few real examples). I have known these men and women personally, and the reason they were chosen for those positions was one word—their *attributes*.

It's Really about Turning Your Passion into Opportunity

Throughout the interview process, it's essential that your passion and love for what you do come through. If you can't get jazzed up about the position for which you are interviewing, then there may be one of two problems: the position is not what you love to do, or you haven't been true to yourself when writing about what you love to do!

As the interview progresses, if it's right for you, it should become evident in your demeanor, your tone of voice, your demonstrated angst to land that job.

This is not the time to be shy and coy. Your body language should exude desire and appetite for the opportunity. It should be obvious to anyone that you are very enthusiastic for the position in question (but not desperate—desperation is a different energy).

If you do it properly, then you are turning your passion into cash.

A Good Interviewer Is Hard to Find

It is quite conceivable that as you go through a number of interviews in several companies, you will become quite adept at being interviewed and responding to their questions. There is a sweet taste of success in that, I think, because many managers are not talented interviewers.

Some hiring managers conduct interviews only once every few years, or they are totally wrapped up in their daily routine and have not adequately prepared to see you. In such circumstances, your challenge becomes keeping your patience while they squirm and struggle before you! Mind you, this doesn't mean that you are a shoe-in for the job—the fact that you are a superb interviewee does not ipso facto result in a job offer. In fact, if you don't handle yourself properly and with humility, an unprepared or insecure interviewer may hold it against you that you are "so smart."

Always bring extra copies of your resume to the interview. Some managers have totally forgotten that they have an appointment with you and can't get their hands on your resume, which they saw in their e-mail a few weeks before.

In general, utilize concrete examples and accomplishments. Keep your answers brief and to the point, your responses to questions positive. Ask your questions as suggested above. Thank the interviewer.

Then, as any sales professional will tell you, "Ask for the order," e.g., ask for the next interview. Say something like this: "Now that you've seen how my skills and experience can help you with your business issues, when can I expect to come back and meet other members of the organization?"

Make sure you understand the next steps.

Smile.

How to Handle the Telephone Interview

When you begin to investigate a position you may be faced with a telephone interview. Many times the phone interview comes as a surprise. It pays to do your homework and find out if candidates are going to be screened by telephone. If you find out that such is the case, then there are some things you can do to prepare.

- Keep your resume and information about that company close by your phone so you can instantly refer to it when on the phone.
- The anonymity of a phone interview may seduce you into overfamiliarity. Remain appropriately deferential in the conversation. Everything counts. There is no such thing as "off the record." If you don't want someone to know it, don't say it.
- Allow the interviewer to do most of the talking, if that's their inclination.
- Expand your answers positively beyond "yes" or "no."
- Speak directly into the phone, enunciating clearly and distinctly. Chances are the interviewer is writing, furiously taking notes or even typing into a computer.
- Take your own notes.
- Ask for an on-site interview, for example: "I really appreciate that you took the time to evaluate my credentials for this position. Will you be calling me back to come out to your facility and meet other members of your organization?"
- Smile. Yes, even on the phone, they will "see" your smile.

Here is a story of what happened to me a few years ago. I was finishing up a networking meeting with a colleague at a local coffee shop. As we were getting up to leave, my cell phone rang. The caller identified herself as Ann Maynard, the recruiter from an important Fortune 500 company. I had just applied to that company online only hours before! Ann said, "Can I ask you a few questions?" So I said, "Sure!" thinking that she wanted to set up a date and time for a telephone interview. But as the conversation progressed, it became obvious to me that *she was interviewing me right then and there*. What's worse, about ten minutes into the interview, the coffee shop manager informed me that the shop was closed and was asking me to leave. Covering the mouthpiece on my cell phone, I put on this look of grave concern and pleaded with the shop manager, "Please, it's a job interview, please let me finish, just a few more minutes?" He reluctantly agreed, and I continued my conversation with Ann.

Fortunately, I had done my homework about that company *before* I actually applied online, so that in fact she did not catch me unprepared. I had even researched what they were willing to pay for that position, and when Ann asked me my salary expectations, I was ready with my response, and it was within their parameters.

My telephone interview with Ann was successful, and it was followed with a lunch meeting with Ann, plus six other interviews in person at the company. The point here is you should do your homework and prepare for the telephone interview even before you apply online.

Immediately After the Interview

As soon as you leave the office or building where you had your interview, it's critical that you evaluate the process you just underwent. Take down some notes:

- Whom did you meet? Names and titles.
- What did each of them say?
- What questions did they ask, and why would they have asked that? This points to where their problems are, which you hope you can solve with your skills, experience, and attributes.
- What aspects of the interview went well? Or not so well?
- What was said during the last few minutes of the interview? Was the interviewer really glad to meet you? Did s/he hint or say they'll recommend you for next level of interviews? *This holds the key to whether you will be called back.*
- Always send a thank-you letter. This can be done as an e-mail, but it's a formal e-mail complete with your identifying contact information and signed (electronically). Read the section below, "The New World of E-Mail" in chapter 9.
- After a few days, call to follow up. Again, express your gratitude for the opportunity to interview.

Chapter Summary

The content of this chapter suggests that there are three tools in preparation for the interview. With the first tool, you learned about the first question that you will be asked by the interviewer, which is "Tell me about yourself" or one of its many variants. This question should always elicit from you your elevator speech, but the elevator speech should be adjusted and adapted to the context of the question and circumstances.

This chapter also discussed the purpose of behavioral interview questions, which types you are likely to experience, and how to turn them into a potent portrait of your skills, knowledge, and attributes. It also points out questions that may arise which may feel awkward to you, and some may even be illegal. Suggestions for overcoming them were presented.

In the second part, emphasis was made about preparation for interviews using the *T-chart for interviewing*, which is the best tool to use for practiced preparation. Preparation also means that you need to analyze and be cognizant of the needs of the employer. Tips were suggested on how to educate the potential employer about your contributions and potential value to them.

There are a number of questions that you must ask your interviewer. These questions are followed by tips and tactics for successful interviewing. A long list of do's and don'ts for interviewing was also presented. The reality of rejection and how to handle it was discussed. There was a section concerning how to handle exploratory interviews. The chapter emphasized that the purpose of the first interview is to get the second interview, the purpose of the second is to get the third, and so on.

The section posed the question, what are they really buying? Your attributes! It suggests that it's really about turning your passion into opportunity. After you have interviewed for several opportunities in different companies, you will be very experienced and most likely realize that a good interviewer is hard to find.

You have to be ready to handle the telephone interview, and this chapter has provided some tips and tactics. What to do immediately after the interview is important.

Homework

1. For a target company or position, gather all information and data points from all sources—job postings, telephone interviews, informants inside the company, people connected in some way to the targeted company, Web site information, etc.

2. Using attachment D, the T-chart for interviewing, make a list of what you think are the target company's business problems, their needs or issues; write them on the left side of the T-chart, in order of priority based on your understanding.

3. On the right side of the T-chart, write down your skills and experience that you can quote to the interviewer as potential solutions to each of their business problems.

4. If you don't have skills or experience that you can directly apply to one or more of their problems, then list one or more of your attributes that would enable you to solve their specific problem.

5.   When complete, rehearse your answers out loud. This is key—it's very important that you not only do the intellectual research and write the answers, but that you also *rehearse these answers*. Why? To build neuropathways which will let you respond quickly and accurately to their questions. This is what athletes do to prepare for important competitive events.

Friday, May 25, 2007

You changed my life! You made me put me first, and no one has ever made me put me first. No one ever asked me "And what do you want for yourself?" I'm getting rid of all the people who were hanging on me, feeding off of me, sucking me dry. But you, Luis—you get to stay in my inner circle.

—Rachelle Evans, after she dumped a horrible employer, followed every step of this job search process, and landed a payroll manager position in Phoenix, AZ, her desired destination.

Four

CAREER COACHING 104

The Compensation Discussion

One question I am often asked is, what's the best time in the job search process to discuss salary?

That's a lot like when people ask me, "What's a good car to buy?" Well, the answer to either of these depends on many factors. The question about salary negotiation is difficult to answer because it depends on many aspects of the yet-fragile relationship between you as the candidate and your potential employer. Generally, I think it's counterproductive to say, "Always do this" or "Always do that." My suggestion is simply that *you should be prepared and be flexible* about when and how to discuss salary.

The best preparation for the salary negotiation begins with research of the market pay rate for your desired position *prior* to approaching the employer—even before you draft the cover letter. Once you send your cover letter and resume by e-mail, you might receive a response within hours inviting you to a quick telephone screen where they may suddenly ask you, "And what are your salary expectations?" If you haven't already done your homework, you'll be caught flat-footed and perhaps ruin your chances for a good starting salary or conversely ruin your chances for a second interview (read my story about this very circumstance in chapter 3, "How to Handle the Telephone Interview").

So for starters, make sure that you know the worth of your desired position. Go to the Web and do an Internet search; query various sources and arrive at a minimum, a midpoint, and a maximum for your desired position. Be cognizant that the value of the position can be very different depending on geography.

An accountant position in Hot Springs, Arkansas, pays differently than in New York City or San Francisco.

Do some research about salary information in the Internet for your desired position; then do some simple arithmetic to arrive at the average salary being paid. One good rule of thumb is to throw out the highest and lowest numbers you find. For example, if you are researching salaries for a mechanical engineering position with five years of experience and you find the lowest salary is $28,000 and the highest is $76,000, throw out those two as they are too far apart and are likely skewed by some undetermined factor, and use the other data points to arrive at an average.

What if They Ask My Salary?

In my view, it doesn't matter to me if the employer wants to know your salary *expectations* during the first interview as long as

1. you have had a chance to tell them all that you are worth, in terms of skills, knowledge, and attributes;
2. you have done your homework so you have an informed guess about their pay practices and;
3. you provide them only your salary *expectations*, not your current salary nor your W-2 information.

If they insist on knowing your current salary, simply reply that this information will be forthcoming as the interview process develops further, and if you are still interested in pursuing the opportunity (and thus your negotiation process has begun).

Remember, you are entering this first interview having done your homework, so now you have a very educated guess about what the position should pay. Here's what you should do to get ready for this first interview:

1. Use your network to penetrate the employer (find someone who works there) and understand the kind of compensation format they have, e.g., are they well organized with rigorous job classifications and compensation ranges? Or are they a family-owned enterprise where the big boss makes all salary decisions using her best hunch?
2. Do your Internet homework and make sure you understand the min/mid/max for this position, give or take $1,000 per annum.
3. Know your own numbers, that is, know the minimum that you will accept and the most desirable but reasonable salary you will achieve for this particular position in this geographical area.

In some cases, it is reasonable for an employer to require two previous years of W-2 information when they are trying to verify information you provided *about sales commissions earned or performance bonuses received or stock options granted*. But you should make this available to verify your salary expectations only when it's clear that you are the *finalist*, and that they have an offer pending for you contingent on verification of your income. While it is not illegal for an employer to ask to see one or two W-2s from previous employment, these criteria should apply: (a) you are finalist for the position, (b) it's for a position with high variability in total cash compensation from year to year, and (c) it's necessary in order to confirm your total cash earnings including commissions and bonuses.

Negotiating for the Optimal Salary

I want to be skinny, with a fat W-2
—Karen Mungenast, finance executive

Total compensation can take many forms, and the higher the position within the organization, the more creatively one can approach this important topic.

Here's what not to do. One of my clients was in the process of negotiating his starting salary and total compensation package. He was a finalist for the chief financial officer position at a regional not-for-profit. He became obsessed with a number that he wanted; it was around $104,000. And after much to and fro, he lost the opportunity because of his single-minded pursuit of that figure.

Fundamentally his approach failed because he did not take into account the many forms that compensation can take. Base starting salary is just one form. For a position like his, there was opportunity to negotiate for a sign-on bonus, a better office, country club dues, professional conference fees, guaranteed bonus after six months/twelve months/eighteen months, clerical support, company car, accelerated salary review, larger budget, larger staff, attendance at exclusive senior management or board of directors meetings, performance-based increments, etc. The list is as long as his imagination. But he was obsessed with a specific number, and they gave the job to someone else. He ended up doing financial audits with out-of-state clients, traveling frequently away from his family, which he really didn't want.

So after all this work you've done to get to this point, don't blow it now with an adversarial encounter with your new employer. The process of negotiating starting salary and other benefits commensurate with the position is collaborative, not adversarial. You must see this simply as a problem-solving process, wherein you get on the "same side of the table" with your new manager and try to resolve the issue. This takes creativity and great interpersonal skills—consider it your first work assignment!

Here's another way to view it—you are helping your new boss solve a compensation issue. Be creative and resourceful. Be pleasant and cooperative. Help her/him see that you believe this to be a problem to be solved by *both* of you, so don't just hand over the issue of your compensation and walk away as if it's totally her problem.

If you find yourself on the opposite side of the table, with an increasingly bellicose discussion, ask for a day or two to think things over, a strategic retreat to let tempers cool. Ask yourself, where is the common ground? Have you reached an accord on any aspects of the job or remuneration? If you want more than they are willing to give, can you do more, that is, can you accept other responsibilities so they see your value added in exchange for the compensation you want?

The main idea is to recognize the box s/he is in and to facilitate and problem solve toward what you want.

Salary Structures

Salary structures are compensation policies and formats set by employers. Generally speaking, the larger and more established companies are likely to have salary structures, salary grades, steps within grades, and a set of written guidelines to help managers with salary budgets. The advantage to you as a candidate for a position in a company that has well-organized salary programs is that you can rest assured you will be paid within the defined range for a position. For example if you are a candidate for an IT director position that has been graded as exempt grade 12, with a range of $85,000 to $105,000, you can be certain that you will be paid within that range to start in that position. They will not hire you below $85K, but they will probably not start you at higher than midpoint, around $95K. You probably will not succeed in persuading them to raise the grade. The benefit of a well-managed salary program is that there is discipline and predictability. The disadvantage is that there is little wiggle room.

Smaller organizations usually have less cash or salary budget, but without the constraints of an established salary structure, they can be very flexible with compensation. The advantage to you is that they can quote the position at, say, $75,000, but after they see you, they decide you are worth an offer of $85,000. That's all well and good, for now, until they hire someone else after you at $90K and then you're not happy—because they have no salary structure.

What if You Can't Come to Terms?

Let's face it, you don't have much leverage, particularly if you're unemployed and have no other offers in hand. This is why it's so important to always keep looking so that you can obtain two or more offers and have some leverage at the salary negotiating table.

If you are stuck, mired in arguments, you have to decide among all the competing positives and negatives of the offer and conclude to either work with it or keep looking.

On a positive note for you, it's not a good idea for a company to continually hammer down starting salaries. People hired under such salary practices soon become savvy that there are better-paying opportunities and leave for better terms. Turnover of this sort is a costly problem for an enterprise.

Think broadly. For example some things to take into consideration are opportunities for advancement. While I was in the US government, I was approached by the regional director and asked if I would be interested in switching career tracks from community relations and communications to operational program management. The move required me to take a step back in grade and pay. I took a pay cut of 17 percent and began work as a supervisor-in-training. In that career change, I learned all about supervision; and in less than two years, I had been promoted twice and passed my original salary. More importantly, I was on my way to a rewarding career with much higher pay in management of a multistate region.

Are You a Good Advocate for Self?

Over the years, as I worked in the capacity managing salary and benefits programs, I would sometimes scrutinize salary patterns using regression analysis. It often happened that I would discover that women were making lower salaries than men. I would then set into motion a plan to fix this and eliminate any gender-based discrepancies. One glaring example, believe it or not, was among physicians. In a hospital where I worked, I ran regression lines of salaries for male and female family practitioners and pediatricians and discovered that the men were paid 10-15 percent more than the women. I took my data to the chief financial officer, who had been responsible for the contractual agreements with each physician, and I asked him point-blank: "Why are you paying the women doctors less than the men?" His response was equally blunt: "Because that's what they asked for."

Now, I couldn't let that practice continue because it was an open/shut case of gender discrimination in compensation. So I battled with the CFO and got him to release a large bundle of unplanned cash, and I raised all the salaries of the female physicians to be on par with the men. I fixed the problem, but it did leave the question on the table: why had the women asked for less?

Women are known as sharp negotiators and advocates for many causes. But are they as good when advocating for self? If you are a woman reading this book, then ask yourself if you've been as diligent in advocating for yourself as you have for your favorite charity. And if you haven't, ask for help, ask for assistance from others who are skilled in salary negotiation.

Chapter Summary

In this section you learned the main point, which is that the compensation discussion should not be an adversarial encounter. In fact, you should see yourself on the same side of the table as your hiring manager; and in circumstances of significant pay and perks, you should definitely help your hiring manager with creative thoughts and ideas to make it work for you.

The worst thing you can do is to have the attitude that "it's her problem, let her figure out how to pay me what I'm worth." Treat it instead as your very first business challenge in your new company.

If you encounter a roadblock, think about a strategic retreat. Oftentimes things have a way of working themselves out after a respite.

FIVE

CAREER COACHING 105

The First One Hundred Days

Catch'm in the corner, 'n smoke 'm in the straight!
—LAM

In sports car racing, one of the classic maneuvers to catch and pass another race car is to brake late while racing toward a corner (a curve on the track), get to the corner first, and then accelerate ahead of the other car. But it takes a lot of preparation to do this tactic successfully. What you're trying to accomplish is to catch up to the racer just in front of you, brake "late," meaning slightly later than your competitor as you quickly approach a corner, pass them on the inside of the turn, and then accelerate out of that curve and leave them behind in your wake. Most of the preparation necessary to accomplish this tactic, which a racer will do time and again during a race, is part of all the work done prior to placing the car on the grid at the start/finish line. It's mechanical work on the engine, tuning the suspension, driving practice laps to find the optimal setup for each particular track, and taking into account even the ambient temperature that can affect plans for optimally setting up a car to run in the front of the pack and have a chance to win.

Likewise, when you start your new job, you have to be prepared before you arrive for your first day of work.

Now that you've landed, what's the first thing you do?

This is a very uncomfortable space—the first few days. You need to put together a strategic plan and a tactical plan. You have to do both simultaneously as the tactical plan has to blend with and be a precursor to and a predictor of your strategic direction.

Your 100-Day Plan

I call this process the 100-Day Plan. Writing your brief 100-Day Plan is very important because it serves several purposes:

1. It allows your manager and your peers to see that you are prepared, that you've thought about this new position and you are ready to act.
2. It gives you an agenda so you can sit with your new manager and explain what you have in mind, based on what you've learned thus far.
3. It allows your new manager to give you feedback, on the spot, about your objectives and your approach, which is a form of an early performance evaluation.
4. It ensures that you'll be focusing on the right things, confirms your efforts will be well-spent, and provides a reality check that the plan details are realistic and achievable.
5. It puts your peers on notice that you have your act together.
6. And as a result, now you know what to do—designed by you!

Your 100-Day Plan can / should be very brief, just a couple of pages! If you write too much, no one will read it. Too long a plan would also seem presumptuous, as if you know a great deal even though you haven't yet started. All you need is maybe a cover memo (one page) with a simple spreadsheet attached. The spreadsheet is just a time line or Gantt chart. Using a software tool like Excel, just write down the major projects or activities on the left side of the spreadsheet and some dates across the top, in weekly increments, up to one hundred days (about 14 weeks). Then in the body of the spreadsheet you mark the dates you plan to achieve those objectives.

With your 100-Day Plan, now you are ready for some activities to learn about your new position. Take your plan and proceed as follows:

- **Meet the people around you:** Set up one-on-one meetings with them. After the warm-up questions about the weather, the kids, etc., ask them what they think needs to be done to improve things in the workplace, things that are within your sphere of influence. Show them your 100-Day Plan, test your theories with them, listen to their feedback and adjust your plan accordingly. In other words, ask them how you can help make things better, and especially how you can help make things better *for them*!

- **Get results—quickly!** When you arrive at your new job, you will probably be asked to decide on a number of issues that have languished since your predecessor vacated the position. Sort the issues into three piles: easy decisions, studied decisions, and world hunger problems. Make your easy decisions quickly, so they can see results coming from you. This will be a big help to your hiring manager because she bet on you, so now it's up to you to make her look good! For decisions requiring more study, form a small team of people with process knowledge. Schedule the first meeting to workshop the problem. But problems that look like world hunger are probably just that. Be careful how you become involved in those; they won't be done in one hundred days.

- **Anticipate, anticipate, anticipate:** Look ahead, discuss issues with those around you, and let them see you are accessible and easy to work with. Then use the information you've been gathering to anticipate what's around the bend. Anticipation—making informed guesses as to what lies ahead—is a very powerful strategy. You will look like a genius.

- **Ask for a mentor:** In many companies, this is a general practice—to have mentors assigned to persons new to the organization. That relationship with an experienced incumbent helps the new employee get acclimated and become productive more quickly to mutual benefit.

One of my clients, Cheri Magin, used this book and, after some months of search, landed a job in a small manufacturing company. We had coffee so she could tell me how she was coming along. When I told her I was ready to write this section of the book, "The First One Hundred Days," she said she wanted to help. I've included her contribution here—Cheri's recommendations for the first one hundred days:

1. **Be a good listener!** Take every opportunity to learn as much as you can from everyone. Say less, listen more. Listen for the "unspoken" messages. Listen but do not give opinion or affirmation (especially to negativism). The more you listen the more people will tell you. Learn the culture.

2. **Prove yourself.** All your achievements will not matter when you walk into a new job. No one cares what you did in the past. It is critical to show you can make a contribution and get along with people.

3. **Be a team player.** Work with teams on projects and also in social settings, like lunch routines or breakfast clubs, after work social or sports events.
4. **Adapt to the culture.** Each workplace has a different culture. Learning the culture and adapting is key.
5. **Be proactive.** Ask for performance expectations and feedback. Schedule a meeting with your manager after thirty days and discuss how you are doing. Request another meeting in the future.
6. **Look for ways to improve the workplace.** Volunteer for something special that needs doing. Look around and take on a project (that can be accomplished in one hundred days). This way you can demonstrate your abilities and get to know some people.
7. **Be positive!** Find positive people, share some of your time and information with them, avoid pessimists, take walks on your lunch break—take your lunch breaks!
8. **Stay in the networking mind-set.** Keep your resume updated, continue to network, stay in touch with people who have common interests, and be involved in activities/clubs/volunteerism.

Chapter Summary

Overall, it's important to set a good tone in the first one hundred days. Getting to know the people quickly and producing some tangible results are key. Listen more than talk, find some good quick hits to show some results. Leave the larger "world hunger" problems for another time.

Write a brief two-page plan for your first one hundred days. Describe what you hope to accomplish in the first 14 weeks of work. Use this document as a platform for discussion of assignments during the tricky first few months on the job.

Above all, find those people who are willing and able to help you and listen to them.

Six

TACTICAL SUPPORT

Unemployed?

Jobs are mortal. Yes, that's right—they are born and they die!
So mourn your job loss and then move on.
—Ann Maynard, Vice President, Human Resources, Blue Tie, Inc.

Many a career has come apart on the shoals of layoffs, plant closures, budget cuts, failed mergers, deep recessions, flat top line revenue (sales revenue), cheaper labor offshore, and many other reasons. If you are one of those who is now unemployed, it is easy to fall into traps of self-pity, procrastination, recrimination, and other conscious or subconscious attempts to challenge reality. The good news is that there is an antidote to this paralysis.

First, give yourself time to heal. Losing a job, particularly after working for one company for many years, is one of the most traumatic events in life. Your grief won't be over by Monday morning. Like the law of the farm (plant in spring, harvest in fall), it takes time for this wound to heal. But you can't just descend into a bed of depression and self deprecation, so here are some suggestions derived from the combined experience of hundreds of people I know who have gone through this. Friends and family can help, but you also need to go out and meet other people, especially people in the same circumstances. You can share stories and be mutually supportive.

One of my clients, Nancy, had lost her job in a company she had actually created about twenty years before. As her software development company grew and evolved, she hired other people to run it and gave them equity in the enterprise. Eventually, her partners found her to be redundant and irrelevant in the new enterprise. They agreed she would separate; she accepted a severance package and started looking for another job. Nancy and I met, and I began my career coaching process. But there was something in the way. We couldn't deploy the tools that I was sharing with her. Nancy wasn't making much progress. So I asked her one day:

Nancy, have you shaken your fist at God?

What?

Have you had a heart to heart with God and told Him how disappointed and angry you are with Him that you've lost your job? Have you asked God—why me?

With that, she started crying.

I said, *Nancy, you have to let it out. You can't pretend that it didn't hurt, you have to accept that it feels bad, really bad, to lose your job, especially in a company that you created. Now, let it flow, talk to me, tell me all about it.*

The grieving process is real and universal. You shouldn't fight it. That's counterproductive, indeed impossible. Instead, take steps to control the only thing you can control in the grieving process, and that is when, where, and with whom. Pick the right person, go to the appropriate place and time, and then let it begin, let it flow. Until you've done that, you won't be able to face the myriad other difficulties that are part and parcel of an effective job search.

There are many books and articles about the grieving process. Armed with information about the grieving process, you will be better prepared (eventually . . .) to look at your grief objectively, not just emotionally, and be able to know when it's in your way and what to do about it. That's more than we can cover in this book, but suffice it to say that it's there—whether you are an elementary school teacher, a marine drill sergeant, or a chief marketing officer, it hurts to lose your job.

Getting started

The following is required behavior for the unemployed:

- Every day is a workday. From Monday through Friday, schedule your time and hold yourself accountable. Shower, shave, put on your business clothes, and be at your work station from 8:00 a.m. to 5:00 p.m. at minimum.

- Create in your home a work space that is solely dedicated to your job search—even if it's only a card table in the corner of your bedroom—when you go there, you are at work, not to be disturbed.
- If it's 2:00 p.m. and you're still in your bathrobe and slippers, you're in big trouble! Why? You need to be in the mind-set of the office, of the workplace, not in your bedclothes.
- Do the laundry, mow the lawn, wash the dishes, and shop for groceries on nights and weekends, as you did when you were employed full time.
- Try to arrange "coffee meetings" for networking in the mornings before work or even after work.
- Make sure you have networking meetings on your calendar. You should have eight or ten each week. Yes, each week. That's not so many. See section "On the Importance of Meeting People."
- Don't ask your network contact for lunch meetings. Lunch meetings require much more time and little gets done amid ordering and eating. Lunch meetings are more likely to be canceled because they take place in the middle of everyone's busy work schedule. Best meetings are before work or after.
- Most unemployed people spend only five hours a week, on average, actively looking for work (according to Lee Hecht Harrison, Inc., a provider of career coaching services). You need to spend six times that to be effective.

  - In your city, there should be a "book of lists" issued by the regional business council. For example, in Rochester, New York, the *Rochester Business Journal* publishes an annual guide to thousands of businesses. In the Miami area, there is the *South Florida Business Journal*. These business publications categorize companies by industry. Get that book of lists for your city. You can look for it in your public library or purchase it at a bookstore or subscribe to the periodical.
  - Read your local business weekly and target companies that are expanding, growing. Then use LinkedIn to find connections to people in the companies you are targeting (Read about LinkedIn in chapter 9). Call one of the senior managers and ask them to meet you for coffee (not for a job interview, for an informational meeting).
  - Plan on making dozens of phone calls each week and sending out cover letters and resumes, at least ten a week.

- If an employer is hesitant to hire you full time, be flexible and offer alternatives—ask for part-time work or work on a contract basis, or even work full time for less than you were working before. Be flexible, particularly as you are at the end of your unemployment benefits. When you get a chance to do the work, do a great job to entice them to hire you.

- Speaking of cash, do you know when you will run out of cash? How many weeks of severance or unemployment do you have left? (I'm amazed at the number of people who don't have an answer to this question.) Draft a spreadsheet containing the number of weeks remaining of unemployment or severance payments. Do a careful analysis of how much cash you need on a weekly basis. Reduce your expenses accordingly; don't run out of cash before you find a job. Be sure to engage your family in these plans; everyone may need to cut back or do without things on a temporary basis.

- When you are looking or work, tell the truth about your situation. Don't be afraid to tell people you were laid off; don't make the mistake I made. Here's what happened to me: I had become unemployed and found an executive search consultant in Boston who was interested in my experience for a good position. I traveled from Philadelphia to Boston to meet her. At the time of our meeting, I had just been relieved of my responsibilities, and I had a generous salary continuance package. Indeed, technically speaking I was still on the payroll and would remain so for a year. When the question "Why do you want to leave your current position as vice president of human resources?" came, my answer should have been, "Because there is a new president, the fifth one in only seven years, and he wants to pick his own senior leadership team, and I have been advised to look elsewhere." That's what I should have said. I can't remember what I did say, but it doesn't matter because it wasn't true. The interview ended reasonably well, and I left the building. When I was walking back toward the train station, I was overcome with guilt, and I walked back into the building. I had to interrupt the nice lady who had just interviewed me, and then I told her the truth. She wasn't happy about what I had done, and I never heard from her again.

- Take a class, volunteer for one or two (not more!) not-for-profits. Try to join their board of directors where you can do good work and meet other highly educated, highly intelligent people. Join a maximum of two not-for-profits; if you volunteer for more, they'll occupy all your time.

- Make sure you schedule some balance in your life—for family, for recreation and exercise (see chapter 10 "Mind, Body, and Spirit")

There is life—during and after unemployment.
—LAM

If you are still employed but trying to make a change, you should be cognizant of nonproductive behaviors.

- It's okay to vent about how much you hate your current job, but don't dwell on it. Vent only with a trusted person who will maintain confidentiality.
- Don't bore your significant other with your complaints about your current job. You'll need his/her input for more important feedback later. Find a good friend or hire a career coach.
- Use your positive energy for your job search.
- Don't procrastinate; it will drain you, and you'll be stuck in a rut.

Opportunity is missed by most people because it is dressed in overalls and looks like work.
—Thomas A. Edison

Don't Look at Rejection

Some people are afraid to go out and try to find work because of the potential for rejection. Rejection is an ever-present possibility when conducting a search, so basically, get used to it. But rejection is not your focus. Your focus is on gathering the data points, information, resources and network to enable your success. That's how you reduce the possibility of rejection and improve the odds of success.

As a track instructor for sports car racing, I often tell my racing students: "If you look off, you go off." Or similarly, "Don't look at the wall—you'll hit it!" It is a physiological fact, especially when driving at 140 mph, that if you look at something with your eyes, your hands will steer you right into it. So in racing, you don't look at the edge of the track while steering into a right hand corner at 90 mph; you look at where you *want to be*, on the track surface much farther past the corner—your hands will take you there.

The Dangers of the Comfort Zone

What would you do, if you weren't afraid?
—Spencer Johnson, MD, *Who Moved My Cheese?*

Beleaguered and Becalmed

Karen White* was working at her checkout register at Wegmans, the ubiquitous supermarket in upstate New York. Karen was in her early forties and was pleasant and conversational as she checked out my groceries on Wednesday nights. I had seen her from time to time, and while chatting with her, I learned that she liked jazz, so we often made small talk around that topic.

One evening, as I went to her register, I noticed that she was quite despondent; she didn't want to engage in the usual chatter.

Karen, are you okay?

Well, no, not really.

How can I help?

I'm having a very bad time. I'm holding this job and two other part-time jobs. My husband and I are not getting along, and I have two girls in high school, and I just don't know what I'm going to do.

I learned that Karen was in the process of getting separated from her husband, and she was trying to keep it all together with paying bills and supporting her two daughters. Karen was very distraught.

Look, Karen, here's my card. I provide career coaching services. If you call me or send me an e-mail, we could get together for an hour, and maybe I can help you get a better-paying job so you don't have to work three jobs, okay?

Okay, I'll send you an e-mail.

A few days later I received an e-mail. The sender was *Mom_slave@ [emailserver].com*. I scratched my head. Was this a prank? Who would name herself Mom Slave? Implications about the sender's psyche came to mind—who is this that evidently feels so poorly about herself? Why would someone announce that she's a slave to her children or to others? In just a few seconds, a torrent of suppositions and conjecture flooded my mind.

I opened the e-mail, and the sender identified herself—Karen White.

Karen wanted to take me up on my offer for some career coaching, and we agreed to meet in a coffee shop.

I confess that it did not go as well as I had hoped. I interviewed her in my usual way, but her demeanor was such that she thought she didn't even deserve that anyone should try to help her. As I proceeded with my usual questions, it became evident that she had come to believe that she had no skills, and that she did not have much to offer. We took longer than usual to get some information down about what she loves to do, her skills, and her attributes. I remember she wrote very little about herself. Maybe it was situational, given her current state with the crisis in her family. But I suspect that it had been going on much longer; for example, her e-mail address, Mom Slave, had not been made up recently. I believe she had had this e-mail address for some time, evidence of a longer term condition.

Karen promised me she would do the homework for Career Coaching 101. Some weeks went by, and I had not heard from her. I looked her up at the Wegmans store, but they told me she had resigned. I lost track of Karen. But I think of her from time to time and of many more like her who have met with me, spent one or two or more hours working with me, but to my knowledge didn't change anything. They haven't done anything different, so they can't move out of their familiar zone nor advance from their current state.

Was it my process that didn't work? Is it this book and its method that failed them?

I think not.

With all due respect to them, I think it was not the failure of the method or of the coaching process.

One observation I have made over the years is how people settle into a comfort zone and remain there in spite of predictable and often dire consequences.

Comfort zones take as many shapes and configurations as there are circumstances in life. Some people fail to educate themselves sufficiently and later in life have the consequences of poor-paying jobs or chronic unemployment. Others stay in very unpleasant or even counterproductive occupations with terrible managers or working conditions because they are afraid of change, afraid of what might be.

> *If you're going through hell—keep going!*
> —Winston Churchill

The example presented by the story of Karen White has many parallels. I'll cite two more.

Comfort Zone Disposition = Disastrous Consequences

Back in 2003, I started a car and boat repair business with two other partners. One partner, we'll call him Rodney, was the factory certified automotive and marine technician. In our partnership, he was the seasoned service manager responsible for running our ten-thousand-square-foot facility and supervising all other technical assistants. The third partner, Jason, was a professional sales representative with a great deal of automotive sales and service experience. Jason's responsibility was to be on the street selling to other smaller dealers and service shops to increase our business-to-business, as well as retail customer base.

My responsibility was to take care of all the administrative, banking, legal, regulatory, and personnel issues.

At first everything ran pretty well, and by early 2004, we had so much incoming business that we hired seven other people to handle the work flow. We noticed that Jason was spending a lot of time in the shop working on cars and giving mandates to all the other technicians, instead of putting feet on the street to drum up new business. Since we were doing fairly well, at this point it appeared academic to address it, so we didn't pursue it. But consequences were soon upon us.

Two things became apparent over time—our employees were turning over very quickly, and our customers weren't returning, even though we were literally gaining one new customer every day, seven days a week. After much review, Rodney and I realized that Jason was not doing any selling; in fact, he spent a lot of time mistreating the employees and mishandling the customers.

We sat down with Jason, explained our findings, and asked him to go out every day and sell. But he didn't want to. He kept coming into the shop every morning, working on cars until after lunch, and then doing a very poor job of looking for new business. No matter how much we emphasized the fact that winter was coming in 2004 and we needed him to build us a reserve of automotive and boat repair projects to get us through the long cold winter in Rochester, he wouldn't budge.

Finally, in November I sat down with Jason.

Jason, here we are again, having this same discussion. Your responsibility in this partnership is to sell, and you haven't brought in any new business in weeks.

Jason said,

Well, I've been out there, believe me, and here's all the places and people I've been talking to.

I could see he wasn't getting the point.

Yes, Jason, I see your handwritten list of names, but that does not constitute a prospect list. That's just the people you happen to know. Jason, you have to extend yourself to this whole market, which is four contiguous counties, especially in the profitable market for boat maintenance and repairs. We need to sign several large restoration projects to work on and carry us through this winter.

Jason protested,

Look, I'm going out every day and trying.

Exasperated, he left me no alternative.

Okay, Jason, here's the bottom line. We have been paying you out of operations. But the problem is that we have not had enough revenue from operations, and I have been writing personal checks to cover the difference. So effectively, I have been paying you out of my personal wallet. No more, Jason. This coming month, in December, you will be paid only from what we earn as gross margin from all the sales you personally make. So if you don't sell anything at a profit, we have no paycheck for you in December. Do you understand?

Jason understood. But astonishingly, he did not change one iota of his behavior.

In December 2004, he didn't sell anything, so we didn't pay him. He quit the business in January.

What point am I making? What lessons can we draw from these few examples? The main lesson that I've learned from observing the behaviors and experiences of some of my clients—and from the loss of my business—is that some people will continue to behave exactly as the day before, within their comfort zone, in spite of predictable and calamitous consequences for themselves and their dependent families. Jason had defined his comfort zone—he just wanted to come in and work on cars at his convenience; he wanted to boss the other employees around even though it was counterproductive, and he wasn't bringing in any new business. But Jason refused to change his behavior even though we had made the consequences eminently clear. He quit the business and went home—unemployed—and owing many thousands of dollars as a partner of a failing business!

A Mole in His Hole

Here's one more example. One day one of my colleagues at work shared with me that her husband, Phillip,* with a doctorate in natural sciences, had been laid off nine months before:

Cherie, what was Phillip's position when he was laid off?*

He was teaching biology at the college.

So is he looking for another teaching position?

No, he's not looking at all! He goes to the basement every day and works with his woodworking tools making custom cabinets and furniture. Then when he sells that stuff to his customers, he barely gets what he paid for the wood, so he's making zero money and not looking for a job. I'm so frustrated with him!

Have you given him my business card? Have you told him that I can help him with career coaching?

Yes, yes, I've brought it up so many times, he gets mad at me. But he won't budge! He thinks that just e-mailing his resume once or twice a day is all he has to do. Meantime, I've had to go back to work to keep our health care benefits, and I'm supposed to be home raising my children!

Cherie, what are you going to do?

I'm going to take my two boys and leave him.

I was stunned. There were wedding photographs of Phillip and Cherie on her credenza in her office. I had known Cherie for several years, and here she is telling me that she's going to leave her husband of six years. I scrambled for an answer.

Cherie, we've been invited to a Christmas party next week, and I know you and Phillip were invited too. Do you mind if I approach Phillip at the party and see if I can persuade him to come to see me?

*Go right ahead. I've done all I can. He is so hardheaded. I'm done with
him. See what you can do.*

At the party, I approached Phillip and emphasized to him that spending
one hour with me going over my career coaching method might make a
difference. He agreed to meet me the following week at a coffee shop.

We met as agreed, and I conducted my usual interview using the tools in
the first chapter. After some discussion about Career Coaching 101, I asked
him to underline on his resume those things that appeared on his list of love
to do. He tossed his resume back at me and said that there was nothing to
underline.

Zero.

Nada.

What Phillip had just done was to inform me that of all the things he
had done, including his education to earn a PhD in science, of all those
things—there were none he loved to do. He was the first client who ever said
to me that he had never done anything he loved.

His resume was very busy but inscrutable. We started from scratch, which
meant his resume had to be completely rebuilt. It took several days in January,
but we got it done. He started sending his resume out, and in six weeks, he
was working as a project manager for a new company, developing medical
products.

Phillip did not know, at least not through me, how close he had come to losing
his wife and family because of his wallowing in his comfort zone—puttering
around the house and tinkering in his basement making cabinets. He had been
unwilling to take the necessary steps to be in charge of his destiny, to create his
own luck. But fortunately he did turn the corner.

Today, more than two years later, I am happy to report that Phillip has
been promoted twice to senior manager of a new products and the start-up
company that he joined has been making great strides.

And he saved his marriage.

On the Importance of Meeting People

Networking is like the lottery—you have to play to win.
—LAM

You do *not* know where your next job is coming from.
OK, maybe you didn't get it.

You do not know where your next job is coming from!

This is why you have to participate in networking. You must be out there meeting and greeting people. You have to be open and yet discerning to many and all possibilities.

Laura Evans was a single mom, with two daughters, and unemployed for eight months. When we met for coffee, she was approaching the end of her twenty-six weeks of unemployment benefits and was preparing to apply for an extension. She had at this point internalized the process of networking and understood its benefits. That's why she was meeting with me; she had heard about me through networking and was telling me about her credentials, experience, and what she loved to do.

To make the story short, this is how Laura Evans graduated to chapter 5 of this book "The First One Hundred Days of the New Job." Here's Laura's e-mail to me on February 25, 2009:

Hi Luis,

I wanted to share with you that I've FINALLY landed! I've been floating around unemployed for almost a year, and I will begin my new career this coming Monday!

In my last position, I was the director of communications for a site construction company. During my time there, I was fortunate to have interacted with accountants, civil engineers, construction site project managers, heavy equipment operators, mechanics, company presidents, owners, and many salespeople. What a great way to start a network!

One of the people I met at my last job was this guy named Nate. He operated the large machinery like backhoes, excavators, etc. Whenever I visited a job site he was on, we got to laughing and struck up a friendship.

A few weeks ago, I was stopping in at my grocery store and I noticed Nate was snow plowing the parking lot in his big truck. I pulled up near his dozer and waved to get his attention, not sure if he would recognize me. He popped open his door and yelled down "Hey, how the heck are ya?" I told him I was OK, wished him a happy new year, and went on my way.

To my surprise, he followed me into the store and we ended up chatting for a few minutes. When I mentioned that I was still unemployed, he suggested that I get in touch with his sister who worked at a local manufacturing company.

I didn't really think it would amount to much, but the company she worked for was one that I had on my target list. A few days later I received an e-mail from her asking me to send my resume. A few days after that I met with their VP of marketing, and I landed a position as Marketing, Public Relations and Advertising Coordinator of a well known manufacturer only eight miles from my home!

The point is, you never know who you're going to talk to that might be the key person in opening a door for you. I wouldn't have guessed it to be Nate. A few shared laughs that grew into mutual respect did the trick for me.

Thanks for all of your guidance and advice. All of the people I've met since becoming unemployed you have helped to shape my choices, and ultimately helped me to land this dream job. It's perfectly suited for my skill set, the salary is more than fair, it's close to home—and the company is progressive, healthy, and really cool! I'm really excited and looking forward to the challenge!

Keep up your good work. I'm not sure you realize what a gift it has been to have made your acquaintance. Thank you!

Warmest regards,

Laura

There are so many examples like that, I could fill this book with stories just like Laura's.

Here is another example of the importance of networking—this one is my own. It was January 1996, and I had been unemployed for nine months. Part of my networking activities included driving eighty miles once a month to a meeting of unemployed human resources professionals, which was held in Princeton, New Jersey.

During those meetings, we would make photocopies of leads and information about jobs that may be opening up and then exchange them. Everyone was supposed to contribute leads—that was the price of admission. The intended result was that everyone would go home with a copy of what everyone else had brought in. Unfortunately, 99 percent of the leads weren't very useful, but it was a start. Remember, there was no Google or Monster or Yahoo then or even reliable e-mail service. Virtually everything was still done in hard copy in those days.

On the day of that January meeting, I woke up early to find about six inches of fresh snow on the ground. I started getting dressed. My wife said,

Why are you up? Where are you going?

I said,

> *I'm going to the HR meeting in Princeton.*

She said,

> *Why? It's eighty miles away and look at all that snow. The roads aren't even plowed. Nobody will be there.*

I said,

> *I have to go. I can't just sit here. Even if only a few people show, I'll have someone to talk to, and that may lead to something. I'll get an early start, so I can take my time.*

As I drove through unplowed snow from Pennsylvania to New Jersey, I thought about how frustrated I was. I had no leads. I didn't even know who I was going to call on Monday morning. With everyone coming back to the office from the holidays, it would probably be weeks before I could have my next telephone screen or personal interview. I was desperate.

While driving, I was thinking that I would get to Princeton and find no one there. I had visions of just turning around on the parking lot and driving eighty miles back to Pennsylvania empty-handed.

I arrived at the designated place, and the parking lot was full! Incredible. Everyone was there, even with all that snow.

The Two-Million-Dollar Tip

Walking into the meeting room, I greeted everyone there as we milled around and exchanged information. Just then Martha, one of the attendees, said to me,

> *Luis, don't you have experience in manufacturing and with labor relations?*

I said,

> *Yes, I do. I have five years of labor negotiations experience in a large battery manufacturing company.*

Martha said,

I heard that Xerox is looking for someone with your experience.

That was all.

That was the tip.

That was the job lead, in its entirety.

So I thought, *Where is Xerox?*

Remember, I couldn't just run home and jump on Google or Yahoo or Wikipedia to find out more about a company. Instead, when I got home I was off to the library to find out more about Xerox by looking in Dunn & Bradstreet, in telephone directories, among annual reports, and in other dusty books and publications.

I found out that Xerox had a large presence in Rochester, New York. *Rochester?* I thought, *Where is Rochester?* Using phone books, I drilled down until I found some phone numbers.

On Monday morning, I started making phone calls. Eventually someone answered the phone. It was Bill Strusz. I have to mention his name because I was so impressed that he actually took my call! Bill was working in Xerox corporate human resources department at the time (he is now retired). I told him about my work experience, and I answered a few of his questions. He said, "Okay, send me your resume." So I did.

Then silence.

I called to follow up but no response from Xerox.

Months went by. In April, I received a call from an executive search consultant representing Xerox. She had my resume in her hand and wanted me to fly up to New York and meet with her.

Well, the rest is history. I landed an excellent job in Xerox in Rochester, and my work experience there has been the best ever.

What's the point of that story?

If I had not joined the Princeton Human Resources Network . . .

If I had not introduced myself to Martha earlier and related to her my experience . . .

If I had not driven to that meeting that one day because of the snow . . .

If Martha had not driven to the meeting that day . . .

If Martha had not remembered me . . .

If I had not taken her lead seriously . . .

If I had not researched Xerox . . .

If I had not called and persisted until I got someone on the phone . . .

If I had not sent in my resume . . .

If Bill Strusz had not forwarded my resume to the executive search consultant . . .

Do you see the point? Any break of any link in this long chain would have destroyed my chances. But it started with me *joining a network and going to the meetings!*

By the way, take time to remember and be grateful to those who help you. When I was offered the job in Xerox, I sent a large bouquet of flowers to Martha.

> *You meet people for a reason, for a season, or for a lifetime.*
> —Peggy Ann Navajas

I had met Martha for a reason.

Ask for Help

About ten years ago I traveled to San Antonio for a conference. Part of the conference agenda was a golf tournament to benefit a college scholarship fund. In the spirit of participation and camaraderie, I signed up for the tournament even though I rarely play golf (sports car racing is what I do for fun).

Foursomes were chosen, and we went out in the wonderful Texas sunshine. As my foursome approached the first tee, I was quite apprehensive about my large handicap. I was very nervous as I addressed the ball. After a couple of awkward practice swings I took a shot, and the ball snaked through the grass for about twenty yards. The members of my group rolled their eyes in dismay. It was going to be a long day.

We bantered and told jokes as we played, but they could scarcely hide their contempt for my lousy game. My score was triple digits by the fourteenth hole. As I addressed the ball for the fifteenth tee, I asked one of the better players, "What am I doing wrong?" He came to where I was standing and helped me with various tips and advice. Heeding his advice, my shots improved significantly for the fifteenth and subsequent holes. I felt relieved, and the other guys actually smiled a few times.

I asked my helper, "Why didn't you tell me before?"

He said, "Because you never asked . . ."

What a lesson I learned in that instant.

I still don't play golf, but I have improved in many other areas of importance to me by simply looking for help from those who are successful. With very, very few exceptions, successful people are ready to help. In fact, I have found that the more successful the person is, in any endeavor—in their profession, in their sports or hobbies, or in any other aspect of their life—the more likely they are to extend a hand and help.

If you need help, ask for it.

On Collaboration

There are literally hundreds of stories I could relate on the subject of successful networking, asking for help and collaborating. Here is just one more, about accomplishing what you want through perseverance and networking.

In the spring of 2008, I became aware that a local author would be conducting a workshop and book signing in the community room of the Wegmans Food Markets flagship grocery store in Pittsford, New York. I decided to attend the meeting so I could meet the author, get an autographed copy of his book, and meet some people. At the conclusion of the workshop, after meeting the author and purchasing his book, I noticed a lady who seemed to be in charge of the event. I approached her and introduced myself. That was a fortuitous meeting because she was none other than Donna Kittrell, purchasing manager for all books and magazines in all Wegmans supermarkets (seventy-five stores in five states). I explained to Donna, who was very gracious and patient, about the book I had been writing (my first edition of *Getting There*) and that I would be very pleased if I could get an appointment with her to discuss my book and how we could collaborate for mutual benefit. Donna agreed to an appointment, and I was in her office just a few days later.

The preliminary result of my meeting with Donna was a handshake agreement that when my book was published, I could come back and we would work out some arrangement for a book signing event, generate some book sales, and maybe even make a presentation.

My first edition was published in August 2008, and I immediately took an autographed copy of my book to Donna's office.

Months went by, and despite all my efforts, I had not received a response from Wegmans. But I had not given up; I just needed to try something different.

One Saturday morning I was filling up my shopping cart with Wegmans products at the Pittsford store when I happened upon Danny Wegman, the CEO of the supermarket chain. I had seen and chatted with Danny many times at a few of his stores. This time, however, I decided on the spot that I would ask for help.

Ever the sharp businessman, Danny looked at the contents of my shopping cart and inquired about how well I liked them. I answered his questions and then I took the plunge:

"Danny, I have a favor to ask of you."

"Sure! What is it?"

"Well, you see, I've published a book . . ."

"You have?"

"Yes, it's called *Getting There*, here is my card so you can look it up in my Web site."

"Okay, I'll do that."

"Last year, when I published it I met with Donna Kittrell, and we agreed that I could do a book signing here, at this store. But poor Donna, she is so busy! Danny, you have Donna working so hard, doing so many thing for you, she just can't find the time to return my calls or e-mails." I said this all with a smile.

"Oh, no problem! I'll take care of this," said Danny.

On Monday morning my phone rang: "Hi Luis! This is Donna Kittrell!"

Donna and I agreed on a date for me to do a presentation and book signing. I asked Donna how many people they normally got at these events. She said they expected about forty, maybe fifty people. I said, "Oh, we can do better . . ."

Using social media (Twitter, LinkedIn, my Web site, and Facebook) to contact my ever-expanding network, we signed up 107 people, more than double the number expected. Donna was ecstatic! Wegmans actually had to rent chairs to accommodate the crowd!

Here's what Danny and Donna did for me when I did the presentation and book signing on April 29, 2009: they purchased a large inventory of my books for resale; they furnished the hors d'oeuvres and drinks for the workshop participants; they rented extra chairs and provided the space for free; and they assigned several assistants to work the food, drinks, cash register, book display, etc.

In exchange, I brought one hundred people to their flagship store.

The point of this story is—you have to ask for help and find ways to collaborate for mutual benefit.

On Exchanging Business Cards

One of the important rituals of all networking practices is the exchange of business cards.

Now, why would I devote an entire section to this? Well, because

- it's important, and
- many people fail to do it.

Exchanging business cards is important because, when done properly, it breaks the ice in the early part of the conversation, helps both you and your host or hostess to relax, and it can be used to generate questions or comments that are more focused and have greater value than just bantering about the weather. How so? Well, let's take the exchange of business cards step by step, and you'll see how this simple but effective ritual can add value to your job search.

If you don't yet have business cards, then ask around in your community for a printer who will do a good job for you inexpensively. Yes, it's true that you can get really cheap or almost free business cards online, but by purchasing from a printer in your community, you are helping her/him make a living and you are establishing another networking contact and advocating for their business for mutual benefit.

For Networking Meetings

Here's what to do before you go to a networking meeting:

- Make sure you have about a dozen of your business cards in your pocket. Here's what I do: I put my business cards in my shirt pocket (nothing else in there, you don't want a pocket protector full of multicolored pens).
- As you introduce yourself to someone, reach into your shirt pocket and offer them your business card. Women may prefer to keep their cards in a sleeve of a notebook or an easily accessible outside pocket of a purse or jacket.
- Then ask them for their business card. If they give you one, you must *stop, look at it, and read it*. Ask them one or two questions about it. In Asian cultures this is a refined art. What you should take away from that is the recognition that a business card is an extension of the professional entity of the person, to be treated with due respect.
- After a brief exchange of information, put their card in your briefcase or in a special place in your purse (not in the back pocket of your pants and not in your shirt pocket because it will be mixed up with your own cards).
- Ladies will have to be more creative about where to keep their own cards, maybe in a side pouch of their purse or briefcase or in the right pocket of their suit jacket.
- Ladies should not be fumbling through all the contents of their purse, as I've often witnessed, to get down to a card holder at the bottom of their purse. (One evening, at a networking meeting I offered my business card to a lady and she accepted it; then I asked her for her business card, and she actually asked me to hold out my two hands as she emptied the many contents of her large purse into my outstretched

hands until she found a little card case at the very bottom. We just laughed . . .)

- In sum, the motion of retrieving and offering your business card should be smooth and practiced.

After a networking event or exploratory interview, as soon as you get home or back to your office, take the business cards that you collected and write a few notes on the back, such as the date and venue of the event, their sports or hobbies, maybe their alma mater or names of spouse or children, whatever you can remember that will help you later in another conversation with them.

By the way, these business cards you collect are not just for you. They are to be shared with others who from time to time need your help. You should see these cards as a vehicle for helping to connect people. When someone calls you with questions about other people or enterprises, you should be able to refer to your box or folder of business cards and give them two or three names and numbers. Today, you may have a personal communication device, such as a Blackberry, Droid, or iPhone to share contact information. I use my iPhone and easily bring up contact information stored in LinkedIn, which I share with people that I'm trying to help. Remember, you would want someone to do the same for you.

The ritual of exchanging business cards is not very complicated. But I'm appalled at the number of people who, during networking meetings and interviews, actually tell me that they don't own any business cards or didn't bring any. I make it clear to my clients that I expect them to go into interviews and networking meetings armed with business cards, and that they engage in the ritual of exchange as suggested above.

For Exploratory Interviews

When you visit an organization for an exploratory interview, you will typically be introduced by administrative staff to your host or hostess, and then typically you proceed to shake hands and greet them. Be prepared as follows:

- After they ask you to sit down, you should reach into your portfolio or briefcase (and I mean *brief* case) and take out one of your business cards.
- You can then say, "May I give you my business card? It has my contact information."
- Then, after your host accepts it, you can say, "And do you have a business card?"

- If your host hands you a business card, *pause for a moment and read it!* This is an opportunity for you to ask one or two questions about its contents and immediately launch into a conversation.
- The worst thing you can do is to accept your host's business card and stick it in your pocket without bothering to look at it. That's a lost opportunity to start the conversation, and in Asian cultures, that's considered very rude behavior—a diss.

What about Working with Headhunters?

Many ask me what to do about executive recruiters. Should they approach recruiters? What's the likelihood that a recruiter will help them land a job? How good is the reputation of recruiters?

As with any other endeavor, there are mostly good recruiters, but there are a few that can leave one with a bad taste. The main concept to keep in mind when dealing with recruiters is that *they don't work for you.* They work for the hiring manager who is paying them a fee to find and screen candidates.

This means that when you write to a search consultant they're not going to be of much help to you unless they happen to have a search assignment that coincidently happens to require someone with your skills, knowledge, and attributes. If that's the case, you are fortunate, and now you've got their attention.

Among your many activities in your job search you'll have to decide how much time to spend on writing to and meeting with recruiters. There are thousands across the land, and there are hundreds even in a medium-size city. While it's not a complete waste of time to send a cover letter and resume to a search consultant, you have to work it into your overall priority matrix. If you think, however, that by corresponding with a few of them, even the very prestigious ones, all you have to do now is sit back and wait for the phone to ring, you'll be wasting your time.

Working with search consultants is not your first priority. *Networking is your first priority.* Your networking list should include some of the prominent search consultants in your region. If you are already doing a good job of networking and now want to work more closely with recruiters, here is a way to work with them.

If you are going to approach a *contingency search* recruiter, keep in mind that they don't get paid by the hiring company until and unless you are hired. That's why they are called contingency recruiters—because they only get paid contingent on the hiring manager actually hiring a candidate presented by the contingency recruiter. You have to be careful with contingency recruiters. The way they work is like this: if you send them your cover letter and resume and they happen to like it because they think your skills are marketable, they will simply mask your personal identifying information with their recruiter contact information and attach your resume to an e-mail blast to every company they know, in hopes one of them will be interested in your skills and experience. Your entire resume will be visible to hundreds, except for your name and address, and it may actually end up in the hands of your current company's human resources director.

A *retained search* firm behaves differently. They are retained (paid) by the company which has a vacancy, and the recruiter gets paid his or her fee even if the search does not turn up a suitable candidate. The fee is typically 33 percent of the first year cash compensation of the newly hired employee. The downside of working with retained search firms is that you would have to write to a great many of them, in the hopes that one has been retained to look for someone just like you.

By the way, even when a retained search firm calls you, you should be very well prepared. I received a call one time from a female search consultant in a firm based in California. She had heard of me through someone else (networking is always my first priority), and she thought I might be interested in a position as a vice president of human resources for a well-known eye care pharmaceutical company. The headhunter had left me a phone message with enough hints that I readily figured out the client company she was representing. I went through the Internet and researched the company and garnered a lot of information about their governance, complete with the names of the top leaders and even with the name of the person I would be reporting to.

When the search consultant finally caught up with me live on the phone, I began asking her a number of questions using information from the research I had just completed. To my utter surprise, I was way ahead of her about information concerning the reporting relationships, dynamics of the different corporate entities, and implications for the position for which I would be interviewing. The gist of it was that I turned down the opportunity because she, the retained recruiter, did not know that the position in question reported to a vice president of international human resources, who in turn reported to the corporate vice president of human resources, so the position in question was something I would have aspired to about twenty years ago. I even knew the names of the vice presidents and had their bios (which were readily available on their company's Web site), information which I used to quickly educate the recruiter.

If she wasn't embarrassed by this, she had no professional shame. Why my adamant tone? She had been paid a princely sum to conduct a search for an executive and had failed to do even the most rudimentary research about the company's senior management team and was oblivious to information about the persons to whom the vacant position would report. All this information was available publicly on the Internet.

Using Groups to Advance Your Search

Author Richard Bolles, in his best-selling classic job search book *What Color is Your Parachute?* reports that a job search is more likely to be successful (84 percent) when it is done in a group with other job hunters applying the most effective strategies. This rate of success drops by 15 percent when the same strategies are followed alone, without a group.

Dr. Nathan Azrin, PhD, is one of the job search experts who advanced the notion of job clubs, and replicated studies have proven the success of that formula—networking.

According to Execunet (http://www.execunet.com), networking is the primary source for executive search firms for finding candidates. They reported their sources as follows:

- Networking 35%
- Online research, excluding job boards 30%
- Online job postings 29%
- Firm's database/resume files 28%
- Advertising 24%
- Faculty contacts 24%

(Numbers add up to more than 100 percent because a resume can be found in more than one source).

Powerful SIGs

In February 2009, I formed a network for executives in transition. I called it GTEN for Getting There Executive Network. The reason I formed this small interest group (SIG) is because as I looked around in my community, Rochester, New York, I found that there were literally dozens of networking groups (Rochester is well known for this), but there were none dedicated to and strictly for the needs of executives. For purposes of GTEN, we define executives as people with C-level (chief level) credentials and incomes of at least $100,000. In my first GTEN meeting, there were eleven of us. We meet every Monday morning, and the group has been growing at the rate of one person per week. We now have more than sixty members.

What do they get out of it? Why do they keep coming back to GTEN? They keep coming back because there is support and wisdom in numbers. A job search is too difficult a task to do alone. You will need help, so join a group. Better yet, form your own group.

This is what Michelle Polowchak and Amelia Blake-Dowdle did. As a lifelong human resources professional, I had the idea of forming a networking group like the GTEN group mentioned above, but for human resources professionals only. At the time that I thought of it, I had already formed GTEN and had a lot of other work on my plate, so I asked several HR professionals in my community to form a group. No one took me up on the idea. Why? Because they said, "Why would I want to form a group of HR professionals in transition? If I formed one, or joined one, I would have to share my information about job leads with others."

Here is the answer to that fear. Suppose you have three leads, suppose you know about three jobs that are coming open. If you join a group of like-minded individuals, a SIG, and ten people show up at the meeting each with three leads, then you will walk in with three leads, and you will walk out with thirty.

There's power in SIGs.

Amelia and Michelle liked my idea of an HR networking group, and they formed QUEST, a group of HR professionals that meets every Wednesday evening at a local college. The group has been incredibly successful because its members can accelerate their job search with more leads and information obtained by membership in QUEST.

By the way, admission to GTEN and to QUEST is free.

> *Ninety percent of success is just showing up*
> —Woody Allen

Follow Woody Allen's advice: join the group and attend their meetings.

Steps to Lifelong Networking

If you want to know more about networking tactics, you can find and read whole books on this topic. I won't replicate their fine work here. But I will leave you with the substance of my experience and the demonstrable accomplishments of those who have effective networking practices.

How do you go about networking? Put this into practice:

- Every person you meet may lead you to your next job.
- *Join* local professional associations and networks.
- *Go* to their meetings and mixers.
- Join digital networks.
- Read professional journals:

o   identify high flyers (accomplished people or up-and-coming leaders),

o   contact them,

o   try to meet them and discuss your mutual professional interests,

o   ask them about their experiences,

o   and learn from them.

- Volunteer for a professional project—doing research, making phone calls, analyzing data, writing reports, etc.
- Bring value to the networking meeting and reciprocate—be a giver of tips and leads, not just a taker.
- Remember to show gratitude to those who are helping you with tips and networking contacts.
- Send your contacts and networking friends an e-mail from time to time, let them know how you're making progress, and ask them how *they* are doing.
- Make sure you respond to any e-mails or phone calls from networking contacts to express appreciation. That's what *you* would want!
- Keep in touch even when people move out of town. They still know a lot of people where you are. And if they moved to another city to start a new position, it's the right thing to do to show some concern for their well-being.
- Seek to become the best connected person in your career track, e.g., whether it's in marketing, taxation, fashion design, finance, imaging science, bioethics, computer engineering, or whatever your field of work is—seek to become the "go to" person.
- Use discernment, consider the source and circumstances of leads that are given to you but generally *follow up on every lead.*

The only statistic you need to know is, how many people do you know,
and how many people know you?
—Tracey Aiello, founder, the August Group

On Networking—an Expert's Viewpoint

NETWORKING
Then, Today and Tomorrow
By Sue Schnorr

In the past, networking was known as a job hunting tool. It's what you had to do to get a job and a lot of people disliked it.

Now, networking has become a core professional competency. Professionals at all levels use networking as a way of doing business; it's not a chore on their to-do list. It's something that positions them to do their jobs better. A tightly-knit circle of friends, business-people and community members is a network. 'Networking' is the process of cultivating mutually beneficial relationships with people in your circle, including fellow employees, clients and vendors, as well as the community at large.

Networking has become an essential skill for gaining a competitive edge. With access to people, resources and information, people these days don't need to be a 'lone ranger'. Professionals around the world collaborate and share resources in order to gather information and gain access to best practices. Working together lends itself to doing a task in a faster, bigger and better fashion. Networking is a two-way street of giving and receiving. Abundance roots itself in networking. When you give, something comes back to you; similar to a boomerang effect.

In today's competitive marketplace, people across all levels (horizontal and vertical) of organizations use their skills to strengthen relationships, make better and quicker decisions, and are more productive and efficient.

In the future, face-to-face networking will continue to be an integral part of a successful workplace. It will be increasingly integrated with social media. It's hard to predict the exact direction it will take, because of the fast-changing environment we live in. But one thing is certain; networking will continue to be the catalyst for deepening relationships, and developing successful, efficient and productive work situations.

Contact Sue Schnorr: http://www.training-insights.com

Visualizing the Ideal New Job

Athletes know the value of visualizing. Their coaches train them to visualize details of their performance as if they were actually doing it to enable neurophysiological changes and adaptations, which they will need in actual performance.

As a high-speed motor sport instructor, I use visualization as a technique to practice my own driving techniques—right in my living room! On occasion I sit in a chair, close my eyes, and visualize myself driving my race car at the track. It's important in visualization to include every nuance, every detail. In my case it's getting in my racing seat and adjusting all my safety gear—racing suit, helmet, harnesses, gloves. Turning on the engine, warming up the oil and lubricants, checking all the gauges, easing into first gear, and driving through the paddock to the pits. Then driving out to the pit lane picking up speed in second gear and easing into the track surface in third gear, up the fast right hander climbing the esses at Watkins Glen International Raceway for my warm-up lap. I will do this in my mind for about "three laps," thinking about every turn, every gear change, every braking zone—driving "the perfect lap" in my mind.

The point I'm making here is that the more you can visualize exactly what you want, the greater your chances of increasing the possibilities that this is exactly how things will turn out.

Visualizing, in my experience, has two critical aspects:

1.   visualize exactly what you want, and then
2.   *tell people about it!*

If you don't know exactly what you want, then it helps to visualize because in order to accomplish that, you must first do the homework to ascertain what it is that you want in your professional life. By the way, visualization works in many other aspects of life, and it works particularly well for interpersonal relationships. There is a lot more than can be said about visualization techniques, but that's outside the scope of this book.

For purposes of this book and career coaching, the result of your visualization should be a facsimile of an offer letter from the president of the company of your dreams, announcing to everyone that you have been chosen for the job of your dreams with the title and salary of your dreams. For maximum effect the "offer letter" should look as real as possible. It should convey every detail of your career aspirations.

Visualization is not silly. This technique presents a very effective way to help you understand exactly what you want, in the best terms and conditions imaginable to you. This "offer letter" that you're going to type up and hold in your hands should provide you with psychological and emotional support in your career journey, for this document conveys exactly what you want at this point in your career.

But I haven't yet convinced you? You still think it sounds silly? This book that you are now holding in your hands, during its inception, was nothing more than a visualization; actually, it was just my idea of the title page, which later became a concept, then an outline, then a basic manuscript, later a completely edited manuscript, a prototype hardbound book and finally a book for sale nationally through major booksellers.

This tangible book is the direct result of my visualization.

> *These tools are part of the collective unconscious. Lives can be transformed if people act on these tools.*
> —Jennifer Sertl, Coach to Executives

Here is another example of visualizing in my career. I was once reassigned to a position within a company. I didn't like the new position, the new office, the town where I was being reassigned, not even the nature of the work involved. This caused me to go into a mental funk. But I didn't stay there long because I knew that I was the only one who could get me out of it.

To make way for myself, I visualized my new position in the best possible way. I wrote a two-page document which on the first page described the way I would furnish and decorate the office. This may seem trivial; but given that I would spend ten hours a day, every day in that physical space, I wanted to make sure that it was optimal. I also wanted it to be the best-looking office in the area, which I knew would have the effect of drawing other people with positive energy. On the second page I described the various ways that I would attack the job content, my desired conceptual outcomes of the position, and even the acclaim from others who one day would describe my work product.

The second thing I did was to show that letter to some people that I trusted but were not directly involved in my line of work or even on my work team.

Third, what happened was that within eighteen months it all happened exactly as I described. People then commented that it was the best-looking office in the area, and they liked to come in to sit and chat and eat some of the Godiva chocolates that I would always have on hand.

Everything in that visualization document has come to pass, exactly as described, including the fact that I've already left a legacy of new processes and initiatives in my line of responsibilities that had never been attempted in that company before.

Visualizing My Book at Wegmans

In my iPhone I have a photo of my (first edition) book on the shelf at the Wegmans supermarket flagship store, in Pittsford, New York. The reason I value that photograph is because it exemplifies three concepts coming to life: visualizing, networking, and asking for help.

There was a time, just a few years ago before my book was published, when all I had was a mental picture of my book. I visualized what my book would look like. At the bookstores, I would go to the career section and look at the hundreds of books available on career topics. Over time, after looking over and purchasing several books on career topics, I settled on a book that had the physical properties of the book I would want to hold and purchase. That book, conceptually, became my model, and with a lot of work with my publisher and cover artist, I was able to put together a prototype. Visualization of that finished product and telling people about my mental image of that published book for sale in bookstores—and in Wegmans—became a mission.

Once my book was published, it became available in Amazon and by order at Barnes & Noble and Borders. But I was not satisfied. I wanted my book for sale at Wegmans. This was very important to me because Wegmans is a business of iconic proportions in upstate New York. With a vision of my title for sale at the flagship store, I plotted my route to success.

Visualizing in Great Detail

I often ask my clients for life and career coaching to visualize what they want, in great detail. Depending on the age and personal circumstances, I may ask a client to visualize what they want in ten years, in five years, in two years, by next Thanksgiving, and even by next week. For example, I had one older client who had built a lucrative multinational information technology enterprise. He was in his early '60s when we were meeting. I asked him, "Think about this, should the next ten years look like the previous ten years?" He answered, "Heavens no! I need to do something different by the time I'm seventy!" But he didn't have a plan. So we worked on visualizing what he wanted to be doing. I asked him this: "It's Tuesday afternoon in June in 2019. What are you doing?" I asked him to take that question back to his family and discuss it. After several sessions we arrived at an answer to that scenario, much to his satisfaction.

Here's another example of a shorter visualization period. I asked one of my clients, Linda Tufts, to envision what she wanted to report to her family by Thanksgiving Day, which was about six months away. The assignment I gave her was to write down the answer to this question: "Linda, let's pretend it's Thanksgiving Day, and you've gathered with your family and friends for Thanksgiving dinner. One of your family members turns to you and says, "So, Linda, what's new with you?" Please answer that question, in writing, so you and I can evaluate the answer, and then we'll use it as a plan."

To be honest, Linda did not like that assignment. She insisted the answer to my question was "in her head," and she resisted putting the answer in writing. But I didn't let up the pressure because there was something there that I wanted to get at, and then I told her what I thought was the source of her resistance. But more on that after this. Linda finally said she would write something over the weekend and send it to me. Here's what Linda e-mailed back to me.

Happy Thanksgiving to all my family and friends and mentors, as you know this has been a challenging year for me but also a year of profound growth and rediscovery of the self—who is Linda? As you all know I was laid off this February, but in classic Linda form, I embraced my unemployment and discovered the limitless opportunities that until February I had not dared to explore. In June I was offered a position as an IT software development consultant, an opportunity that was literally designed for me by my new company, Awesome S/W, Inc. Those that have worked with me over the years had always advised me that I was made for consulting; I finally listened to those who love me and jumped in with two feet and one big splash, arriving in the nick of time for s/w development systems.

I am a little embarrassed by my salary and compensation package that I received from Awesome S/W Inc., sometimes with all the on the job training I am receiving I think I should be paying them—not! I asked for and was offered $92,000 annually and in addition, was given 50 shares of Awesome S/W stock with additional stock purchase options, dental, medical, 401(k) with matching at 50% by Awesome S/W, effective immediately; 20 days of paid vacation plus an additional 6 for holidays. I invite you to visit their website, they have fingers in many markets and have positioned themselves for success and I am a big part of that, www. awesomes/w123.com.

There is also a method to my madness and although I have caused a great deal of concern for my parents, family and friends with all the job changes since moving to Rochester each one was designed by me to further position myself as the expert in the IT field and it paid off, big time.

I am living in my favorite city of Rochester NY. The things that I have learned, and the team that I work with is bar none greatest professional experience of my life, I am truly blessed and thankful this Thanksgiving season.

My dog is doing well, she misses me so much during the days when I travel, but has grown accustomed to living with my dog-sitter. She is still the best companion that I have ever had, and we make the most of our time together.

Happy Thanksgiving, I love you all!

Linda

The above example demonstrates how you should visualize, which, in order to be most effective, should be in great detail. Linda could have done even more, for example she could have described her office, and the quality of relationship she would have with her manager and peers. If you visualize in great detail, then you actually increase the possibility of arriving at exactly that desired objective.

It's counterintuitive. Most would say that by having just a vague idea is sufficient, especially to remain open to many and all possibilities. We say that, but then we behave in just the opposite way. If you need cardiac bypass surgery, then you find an expert, a surgeon who is totally focused on open-heart surgery; you want someone who is board certified in that subspecialty and has done literally thousands of procedures. You don't lie on an operating table to have your chest cracked open by a general practitioner who has been keeping his medical practice options open.

Preemptive Buyer's Remorse

Buyer's remorse is that unpleasant sensation of regret after having purchased something. It could be as simple as getting pistachio ice cream, then regretting not having chosen chocolate. Or more significant—like signing for a new red convertible without asking your husband. But why talk about buyer's remorse in this book, at this point? And what is preemptive buyer's remorse?

If you recall from above, Linda had resisted writing down her visualization of a new job. As I explored through conversation and questions the reason for Linda's resistance, it came to me. So I asked her, "Linda, for the last few weeks you have declined to write down you vision of the ideal position. You've told me that it's in your head. But I want to see it in writing. Why don't you want to write it? *What are you afraid of?*"

She didn't respond, but her skin color changed on her face, so I knew I was on to something. I said, "I know what you're afraid of."

She said, "You do? What?"

I said, "You are afraid that you'll visualize and write down 'the wrong job' and that you'll find it, get it, work it, and then in six months realize that you've made a mistake. Isn't that right?"

She said, "How did you know?"

My name for this pattern of behavior, which I see on occasion with some clients, is *preemptive buyer's remorse*. It's an unconscious inability to commit to a destination. There is a logical reason for this. If I ask a few questions I quickly discover in these cases that there is a history of the client "getting it wrong," that is, that they have accepted a position in the past, without really understanding what they want, only to discover later that it's the wrong position.

But here's the paradox—if you choose to focus and identify what it is exactly that you want, then you significantly increase your chances that you will get the "right job" and then you won't have to worry about buyer's remorse. It's counterintuitive, and to be honest, it is often a major obstacle to progress for some clients in their job search if they insist on "being open to all possibilities." If you remain "open to all options," then you are simply making it more difficult for others to know exactly what you want. By remaining open to all options you thereby make difficult for others to advocate for you and for potential employers to discern where in their organization they may play you.

Here's another way to say it. Playing not to lose is a totally different mind-set than playing to win. Using sports car racing as a metaphor, you drive to win, not just to finish the race. Now, there may be times when your car is not working optimally and you have to "nurse it along" to finish the race, but that's the exception. No one goes through all the trouble and expense of racing to show up at the race track just to finish. Every racer does all their preparation work and they practice, they make adjustments to their racecar and then they show up to win. So should you.

Performance Management

Not everything that counts can be counted, and not everything that can be counted counts.
—Albert Einstein

While you're engaged in your job search, or in your effort to be promoted or to change careers, you need to understand how well you're performing, how effective you are. In order to understand what you've done and what remains to be done, you should keep score in some way. Now, as Einstein said, the mistake to avoid is that not everything that can be counted counts. This means that although it's easy to count, for example, how many telephone calls you make in a day, this easy performance measure doesn't help you if the phone calls you've made are to companies in environments not compatible with your skills, experience, and attributes.

Conversely, the quality of some telephone contacts or even interviews are hard to measure, but in fact may carry much more impact and have better predictive qualities, even though those dimensions are difficult to count and characterize.

But measure you must.

Use Excel, if you can, or just a handwritten chart that you can use to track your progress.

- List networking contacts, with name, address, contact information, notes regarding most recent conversations.
- List organizations contacted, positions applied for, decision makers and recruiters contacted. It's imperative to keep careful notes about what they said so that if there is further contact you can be impressive with your data and project management skills.
- List interviews, with names and contact information of all persons you met, and notes about each.

By the way, this is not just for your benefit. This is also information that you will use to trade with others in the same circumstances. The better your information gathering and database, the more valuable your "currency," as you go to market to trade with others and help them achieve their job search objectives.

Top 7 Characteristics of the Best

Someone brought this list to my attention, and I have found it very inspirational, and practical. I have posted it prominently in my office, and I read it from time to time. It contains just the right amount and quality of content and inspiration.

Make these your own top 7 characteristics:

1. **The Best have vision:** They can chart the future, can visualize what others can't, or won't. They work hard in the present for the desired result in the future. They go forward with strategic intent.
2. **The Best are optimists:** The best are eternal optimists, walking a fine line between realism and idealism. But they believe what they want can be achieved. No matter how bad things are, the Best find a way to make things better.
3. **The Best dare to take risks:** They play to win; they don't play not to lose. They will do what others aren't willing to do. It isn't about

elimination of fear. Or waiting until you feel no fear. The Best feel the fear and do it anyway.

4. **The Best focus on relationships**: It was Margaret Wheatley who used science to support her statement: "Relationships are all there is." The Best work with others to achieve their vision. They also help others whenever they can. They respect others and give without the expectation of a return.

5. **The Best are adept at execution**: Lance Armstrong publishes how he trains in his books. But others can't achieve what he did because they aren't willing to execute on their plan. The Best plan their work, and they work their plan. They take action in spite of fear.

6. **The Best make no excuses**: The Worst look for excuses to fail, the Best look for reasons to succeed. When they do fail, the Best do not see it as permanent character flaw, but rather a temporary setback. The Best admit their mistakes and move to their next objective.

7. **The Best leave a legacy**: They work for more than themselves; they have in mind a much broader agenda, beyond themselves. What they leave behind is not just money, but a way of doing things, a grand concept, a dream that became real.

Supersize Your Dream

What do you dream about? What is it that you would like to achieve? What have you been searching for, longing for in your professional life?

In my consulting practice I am thrilled when a client asks me how to reach a higher level. It's exciting to me because it's one of the most rewarding things that I do—to have the opportunity to help those who ask the question, to watch them blossom, to help them on a different path ramping up to a higher level.

I was coaching a chief financial officer of a major manufacturing concern in Minneapolis. I'll call him Henry. Henry had been exploring his current situation and what he should do about it. As a senior executive he had been enjoying a six-figure salary, bonus, stock options and executive perquisites. But he felt he was still lacking something. He wanted a leadership position, but not necessarily in finance. He was weary of closing the fiscal month/quarter/year, over and over. It was the same routine, and now he felt underutilized. I asked Henry a simple question: "Henry, let's say that it's a Tuesday afternoon in November, five years from today, the year is 2014. What are you doing? What do you envision you will be doing on a Tuesday afternoon in November, five years from now?" I waited for his response. He said, "I would be the chief strategy officer for the company."

This caught me by surprise. I found myself scrambling a bit, trying not to look surprised. I asked him a few roundabout questions as I prepared mentally for the question that I really wanted to ask him. I finally found an opening in his remarks, and I said, "Henry, I have one more question about your dream position for 2014." I was very respectful and diplomatic, and I asked him, "Is it big enough?"

Now he was the one who was surprised—at himself. Henry realized instantly what I meant. He had not reached out far enough; he had not thought big enough, he was shortchanging himself from the outset. I then said, "You know, this doesn't mean that you should want to be the CEO. It's not that kind of size I'm referring to. Instead, have you thought about being on your own, putting together a great idea backed up by some capital, which I'm sure you have?" I continued, "Or maybe in a completely different arena, you could start a 501(c)(3) not-for-profit organization to work on a mission you've always wanted to pursue." Henry became very contemplative. He hadn't thought quite like that. "Henry, I see all that you are, all that you have in potential, and may I have your permission?" He said, "Sure!" I continued, "You have a lot more to offer your business community, your family, yourself. You now have an opportunity—to leave a legacy."

If you are longing for something different, something bigger in your professional life, in your personal life, then take time to think about it, maybe write it down, and express your dream. Try discussing it with a trusted friend, with a loved one. Do you have informal advisors or a mentor or a coach? Tell them what your idea is and ask them this: Is your dream big enough? Do they see you reaching out to the extent of your full potential? Are you driving your very best race just to finish—or to win?

Summary

This chapter starts by offering tactical advice and support. And it ends with encouraging you to dream big.

If you are unemployed, your full-time job is to look for work. But first you must go through the grieving process of your job loss. You can't skip that step. When grieving, if you don't have some help from friends, family, and coaching, you may fall into disabling depression. It's important that you focus on your objective and recognize stumbling blocks and diversions. There were examples noted above about people who remained in their comfort zones, did not change their course of action, and experienced disastrous consequences for themselves and others around them.

Networking and asking for help are highly recommended as a means of breaking out of current circumstances. The process of relationship building and asking for help is reciprocal and for mutual benefit. The use of business cards and working with headhunters was explained. Forming and participating in small interest groups was discussed and the power of visualizing was explained, with examples.

Read about and think how to apply the seven characteristics of the Best. And supersize you dream.

Homework

1. Put all your job search activities on a paper calendar. You should have at least ten meetings each week. From each person, you will learn about one or two or three others that you should meet.

2. If you are unemployed, visualize yourself in your new position: begin with an introspective sense of self, then your physical environs, and finally the type of work you'll be doing as well as the type of work or tasks you don't want to do. Write the ideal offer letter. You may have to make some compromises, but at least you know what you want on several levels and dimensions, not just salary and benefits.

3. Write an announcement memo, as if it were from the president of the desired company to all staff, announcing your new appointment. Include in the visualization memo all aspects of the job. Include the ideal salary (this would not appear on a distributed memo, but it helps you visualize the targeted position).

4. The first part of visualization is to be very specific, so your memo should appear to be the real thing. The second part is to share your vision. Show this memo to everyone you trust.

5. Make a sunshine folder for yourself (described in chapter 3).

SEVEN

CAREER DEVELOPMENT
AND DIRECTION

Put on Your Rain Tires and Drive

Watkins Glen International Raceway, Labor Day Weekend, 2008—The world of sports car racers is divided into two camps—those who drive in the rain, and those who won't. Those who won't drive in the rain will say that it's dangerous, it's crazy, or that they've already had an accident in the rain so they won't try it again.

I'm writing this section as a metaphor for realities in life—because the sun is not always shining, the track is not always dry, the temperature is not always 75°F. As a driver, you can't always count on using your racing slicks (sticky racing tires without tread) to race in dry, sunny weather. In life we have cloudy days, windy days, fog, sleet, hail, snow, hurricanes, etc. So my approach to sports car racing—and to life—is to try something different, learn new skills, stretch my boundaries, and make informed decisions in areas outside my comfort zone.

Among sports car racers, I'm in the minority because I've never missed a run group or driving session just because it's raining. In fact, as a result of my experience in the rain, many of my racing students have come back to me over the years to ask me to jump in their cars, ride with them, and give them driving tips. They call me Mr. Smooth Martínez, a reference to my driving style that is silky smooth, not hurried—going stinkin' fast while making it look easy and comfortable. It's a driving style that I've honed and finessed over sixteen years of track time.

Where did I develop that driving style?

Driving in the rain.

During Labor Day weekend, I was instructing for Ferrari at Watkins Glen Raceway in upstate New York. Early that Friday morning it was raining, a steady drizzle, with occasional bursts. When they gave the go ahead for Red Run Group to go out on the track, I suited up, drove out of the pits, onto the main track and up the esses (the uphill, high-speed curves). As I made my way around the track in the rain (wipers going), I made eye contact with every flagger at every flag station. Those men and women are watching every move I make, and they can save me from a bad situation with their expert flagging experience. Lap after lap (wipers going), I incremented speeds in certain sections, driving the car "off line," around standing water puddles, because the normal racing line looked too slick or had running water. I had done five laps (wipers going) in my bright red Porsche 911. Incrementing speeds where I could, I was going up to 100 mph at the short stretch coming up from Turn 7 to Turn 8. In the front straight, I was shifting up to fourth gear and running up to 110 mph. Going down the back straight I was hitting consistently 120 mph (wipers going) in the rain. My driving was a picture of exquisite concentration and silky smooth inputs—acceleration/deceleration, transition from right to left, in soft, subtle, maneuvers; my hands hardly moved, my pedal work was pillow soft to prevent upsetting the chassis, keeping the car moving swiftly but safely.

After the chicane, racing downhill and turning right into "The Chute," then left into "The Laces" (an altitude drop of eleven stories), I braked for the very tight right hander, known as the "Toe of the Boot," which ironically is the slowest point on the track. Having completed my braking, heel-and-toe and downshifting to third gear, I cleared the apex on my right and slowly applied gas to go up the hill. But it must have been too much gas where the rainwater drained from left to right; the track condition had changed since my previous lap. The back end of my car came to my left, I steered left to catch it, then it swung right, and I countered, then it swung wildly left again and turned me completely around so I was going up the hill backward! Both feet in (on clutch and brake) I was all locked up sliding backward—uphill. In what appears like a slow-motion movie, I was looking out my left (driver's side) window at the blue steel wall going by, only a few feet from my door handle. The front left tire then touched the grassy edge, lost all traction, whacked the Armco with the front left fender and then bounced back to hit the left rear corner. My car quickly came to rest on the grass, facing downhill. I found myself looking down the hill (wipers going) at the flagging station I had just passed, about fifty yards away. I stretched out my arms, like a big T, to signal to the flagger: "I'm okay. Send the tow truck."

The left front fender was bashed, and the left taillight was broken, but my car was drivable, so I drove it up onto my trailer and towed it home. The next morning I drove my Jeep back to the track to be there among the drivers and Ferraris and help with on-track instruction. Chatting up the racers on Saturday and Sunday, I found the racing camp is still divided. There are those who insist that I was a fool to go out in the rain. But it was my first shunt at the track after driving for sixteen years, and there were others who said, with a grin, "You've graduated!" to the society of those who have crashed at the track.

Despite the controversy, I'm a firm believer that you become a better driver in the rain.

By the way, there were several Ferraris that crashed that weekend at the Glen. All those other accidents happened under perfect track conditions and sunny skies, except one (wipers going).

What's the lesson here? What does this have to do with career decisions? Each of us, in a free nation such as we enjoy, have a multitude of opportunities in our career choices. Using discernment to make reasoned judgments among the opportunities is critical. Making informed decisions is vital.

But once in a while, you just gotta put on your rain tires—and drive!

"If you don't walk back to the pits with the steering wheel in your hand once in a while, you ain't really trying."
Mario Andretti, world champion racer in Formula One, Sports Cars, Indianapolis and all imaginable types of auto racing

"Open" and "Closed" Vocations

There are some occupations that are "closed," meaning that you cannot perform them because you are not credentialed or licensed. For example, pharmacist, commercial plumber, school psychologist, policewoman, stock broker, dental hygienist, commercial real estate appraiser, corporate counsel, etc. You can only pursue those careers if you obtain prescribed training and associated credentials from third parties who officiate over these educational and practice requirements.

The good news is that there are many more occupations that do not require prescribed education, credentialing, or licensing, for example: chief marketing officer, recruiter, Web developer, payroll manager, systems analyst, administrative assistant, event planner, translator, fund raising director, vice president of operations, etc.

These open occupations, as I call them, afford you countless opportunities for growth and professional development. That's not to say that closed vocations do not lead to growth, but that the growth is at times restricted or constrained by credentialing requirements.

In either case, the path to progress is based on developing and demonstrating a deep (vertical) subject knowledge base. So if you are a network engineer, for example, you would want to immerse yourself in the subject to develop expertise and credibility. Armed with this credibility you can aspire to more responsibility and greater scope of authority—in exchange for promotions and salary increases.

I don't need a concrete sidewalk to get across. I just need some stepping stones.
—LAM

Why do I state the obvious? Because oftentimes, when a client is stalled in their career and wondering what to do next, they manifest a deep longing to go back to college and get a bachelor's or a master's degree in a totally new field.

While desiring to increase one's education may look, on the surface, to have merit, the plan often falls short when submitted to scrutiny. They are, in this case, acting more out of desperation, reaching out to whatever solution seems plausible. They sometimes achieve that new educational level only to discover—after significant expense and several years of toil—that they are in the same place as where they started.

Here's a better solution, which I call climbing the Ts.

Climbing the Ts

Let's use my wife's career path to illustrate this concept. Sharon changed careers several times and is eminently successful in a totally new field—information technology—for which she has had absolutely no formal training. How did she do that?

Applying the concept of climbing the Ts we can chart when she was climbing the vertical aspect of the T, e.g., learning more and more about a specific subject, and when she moved over to begin another career path, on the horizontal aspect of the T.

When Sharon was in high school, her parents wanted her to be a secretary, taking courses in typing and stenography. But Sharon had other plans.

After graduating high school, Sharon went back to high school, for a thirteenth grade, to pick up the necessary precollege credits that she had missed. She really wanted to be a nurse, not a secretary. Sharon then enrolled in the University of Delaware's school of nursing, graduated with a bachelor's degree in nursing, and began work as medical/surgical nurse.

Visualize this: Sharon climbed the first T, the vertical aspect, as she learned more and more about clinical care. She eventually became charge nurse in the cardiac critical care unit, taking care of acutely ill patients. A few years later she decided that she'd rather be a nursing instructor to have more predictable, more consistent hours of work.

At this point in her career, Sharon was moving on the horizontal aspect of the T, reaching out for an instructor position. Her first teaching position was at a hospital specializing in burns. But Sharon knew nothing about clinical care for burned patients. She had to learn it—quickly! Her first year was very difficult, she would read and learn the clinical care aspects of the burned patient one night and teach the material the next morning. It was very stressful, but she succeeded.

Sharon had been climbing the vertical aspects of burned patient care, learning the specialty. She did that for a couple of years, then she moved to another teaching hospital, but this time for a cardiac care teaching position, which was more of to her liking. Again, she climbed the vertical aspect of the T learning more and more about physiology and cardiology.

When a management position opened for director of critical care, Sharon applied and was promoted. She then had to learn to manage hundreds of nurses working the emergency department and in the operating room. Sharon had moved across on the (horizontal) aspect of the T and was now learning the (vertical) subject matter—people management and large complex budgets.

While she was learning this new, complex job, she enrolled in the master's degree program at Villanova University in Pennsylvania. When she graduated, she wanted to apply her master's degree to explore the business side of the health care enterprise. Using her experience, she reached out into a totally different environment and was hired as director of operations for a large for-profit HMO in Philadelphia. Again, she had gone out on the horizontal of the T to learn something new.

Sharon was now overextended with her work responsibilities. In addition, the HMO had run into grave financial difficulties. I saw the stress that she was under, and we talked about it. We resolved that she would go in the next morning and tell the management that henceforth she would be self-employed, as a consultant to them, so she could control her calendar and her work hours. We were prepared for her to come home without a job. But they wanted her services, so they accepted her terms; and on the spot she became a free agent, a self-employed health care management consultant. Sharon had just climbed out unto another horizontal aspect of the T, and now she had to learn how to be successfully self-employed.

The HMO became insolvent, and Sharon shifted her attention as a consultant to a psychiatric hospital facility. Again, reaching out on a horizontal, she had to learn all about psychiatric care, insurance reimbursement, regulatory topics, etc.

We moved to another city as a result of a change in my employment, and Sharon continued to work as a consultant, earning six figures and having to hire an assistant to keep up with the demand for her services. She was climbing the self-employment (vertical) aspect of the T.

After several years we moved to Rochester, New York. There, she was nominated to the board of the e-Business Association while solidifying her vision health care's use of the Internet. In 2004, her work was recognized by the e-Business Association when she was named e-Business Executive of the Year. She eventually landed a position in the University of Rochester Medical Center, responsible for development of the first consumer Web site for the medical center.

When Sharon joined that URMC team, she had a blue sky idea—that the Web was a very powerful tool, and the medical center should use it to market its clinical services and to create functionality in several aspects of its operations.

Sharon's work with the Web rose quickly to the attention of the URMC leadership. They promoted her to director, Web services, enterprisewide, and gave her a significant increase in salary and team and budget to manage.

Sharon went from being an individual contributor to managing a team of eighteen information technology professionals. They are creatively developing software with unique intellectual property and application possibilities for every university hospital in the nation.

In May of 2008, the Association for Women in Computing selected Sharon as IT Woman of the Year.

Climbing the Ts is about agility. It's about anticipating inexorable change, having a vision, solid attributes, and being prepared for the opportunities as they arise. Climbing the Ts is not only rewarding and refreshing, but it is a required ability in today's complex and ever-changing marketplace. As employers become global in scope, every person must be alert to the trends on the horizon. Everyone must be on the lookout for opportunities to climb the T.

Timing Is (Not Always) Everything!

John Yurkutat and Dorothy Byrne

In 1982, I was interviewed at Hay Associates, a prestigious management consulting firm headquartered in Philadelphia. John and Dotty were managers at the firm, and they offered me a position. I started work there in April, sharing an office with a quirky but very bright fellow. Anyway, as the days turned into weeks, I became concerned and frustrated with the lack of content of my job. I felt that all I was doing was reading and assisting some of the consultants. One of the operations managers resigned from Hay and John and Dotty put me in her place. The assignment was called manager, project leaders, and I would supervise seven very bright young graduates of prominent colleges in Philadelphia. It was at this point that John and Dotty informed me that they had originally hired me for what I had to offer (my attributes!) even though at the time they did not have a specific job for me until the operations manager resigned. They hired me at a time when our economy was sour and unemployment was high. Arguably, the timing was awkward, in that they did not have a vacancy that I could immediately fill. John and Dotty believed in me to the point of hiring me and placing me on reserve until the right opportunity became evident.

Sometimes You Just Have to Let Go

Don't be my victim.
—Jack Welch, Former Chairman, General Electric

But sometimes you have to just walk away. There are times in our career life when getting up in the morning, we can't bear to even think about another day doing an insufferable job. I have been there. And I have quit without a place to go. *This option is not for everybody.* It requires immense internal and supportive resources. But it can be done.

For example, when I worked for John and Dolly at Hay Associates in Philadelphia I was busy taking care of client requests for compensation and benefits survey data. But the work culture and the management style at Hay was not agreeable to me. One day I came in and wrote a resignation letter. I wrote, "I hereby resign from Hay Associates effective _____."

I intentionally left the date blank on the resignation letter, hoping that I might be able to negotiate some accommodation. Besides, I had no job to go to.

They asked me why I was quitting. I replied,

Look, this is your company, you are the partners and you can certainly run it the way you like. I just can't be a part of it.

Did you get another job? Where are you going?

I don't have another job. Do you want me to clean out my desk?

I thought they would escort me to the elevator and mail me my personal effects. This is what they had done to others. But they wouldn't let me leave. By tendering my resignation, I had taken the gorilla off my back, and I could feel better about work, so I went back to my office and continued working. On my desk was Project 14, the most important executive compensation project that the company had at that time. This happened during the mainframe era, before PCs were evident on everyone's desk. I had been running all the complicated compensation analyses on the IBM mainframe; and all the data, computations, processes, and formulae were in my head and on my desk. I had built enough of a trust relationship with them that they knew I would never sabotage their business.

About six weeks later, Jack Sosiak called me from Exide Battery Company. He had gone there as the vice president for human resources. He remembered me from working with me at Hay and offered me a position as the manager of compensation and benefits, an offer I gladly accepted.

In the above example, I successfully resigned without another job, from a position where I felt I didn't belong. You may ask why I mention Hay in this experience? Isn't that unkind? Well, no, it's not unkind. I don't have any regrets; I learned a great deal from them, and it's a credit to their management that they let me stay and continue working until I found another job. In the end, it was mutually beneficial, and I have always been proud to have been a part of the Hay Group.

Please keep in mind that, as far as I know, at Hay they didn't change any of their practices, certainly not for me. It's important to recognize when to do a strategic withdrawal and not be deluded into thinking that your boss or the company will make changes to mollify you.

But remember—don't be their victim.

On the Importance of Mentors

The most interesting thing on this planet is another human being.
—LAM

Mentors are persons that are interested in helping others. I believe it starts there, with a person who is willing to help. And I believe that the mentee (that's you and me—those who need a mentor) has the burden to look for a mentor. For the relationship to work, the chemistry has to be just right. Both the mentor and mentee need to have the right combination of personality characteristics to make it mutually beneficial. That's why I think it's tough to find a mentor. Mentors are, as we say in Spanish, like *oro molido*, as valuable as gold dust.

Here's a story of a mentor who significantly changed my professional life:

Jack Sosiak

Among the senior consultants dealing directly with the Fortune 500 customers at Hay Associates, there was one—Jack—who was pleasant, confident, and urbane. With a degree from the University of Pennsylvania, his demeanor was impressive. Jack had a rich history of work as a human resource executive with the Campbell Soup Company. I looked up to him and knew him to be wise and savvy. I had not worked with him very much, so my dealings with him were infrequent.

Jack had called me from Exide Battery Company and offered me a position reporting to him as a new manager of compensation and benefits. I accepted the position, and during my five years at Exide, I traveled widely with Jack. He always had me at his side and was always imparting wisdom and factual knowledge about human resources philosophy and practices and about labor relations, in particular. I have never met a better labor relations executive. His agenda always was to establish trust with the union leaders and always pleasantly but firmly work for the mutual benefit of company and union membership. The balance that he maintained and the ethical approach he took to labor relations was superb. I can't say enough about Jack in this area.

But it didn't stop there. Although Jack was ten years older than me, he seemed a lifetime more experienced. And best of all, he wanted to share all this with me. We had long conversations, especially when we traveled (and worked sixteen-hour days!), where he shared with me his view of the HR world. He not only knew a great deal about human resources and labor relations, but he had also visited many cities in Europe and South America and knew good hotels, good restaurants, good food, good French wine and Cuban cigars. I enjoyed every pearl of wisdom that Jack shared with me.

I consider Jack Sosiak as a great mentor. He helped me tremendously. And he didn't really have to.

Chapter Summary

There are many times in one's career that you have to take an informed risk. Like racing in the rain, you take into account all the parameters and go forward with strategic intent. The fact that there are environmental constraints (like rain on the racetrack) should not obviate the decision to move forward.

If you are in a closed vocation, the advantage to you is that you can work in that space, say corporate counsel, or change completely and become chief of operations. The reverse does not work without appropriate credentials. As you explore different options, think of it as climbing the Ts, meaning that you learn a lot about something very focused, until you need a change and look across at other opportunities. Then you choose one, learn a lot about it, and the process repeats. That's how you move from one career to another, over time.

Timing your career move has to coincide with the hiring manager's. This is true whether you are unemployed looking for your next position, or simply angling for a promotion or a transfer. But you have to know when to hold your head high and walk away—without causing collateral damage.

Finally, there is emphasis on exploring for and working with a mentor. It takes time to identify and work with that person, but there are many available who would like to help.

Homework

1. If you are currently employed, think about some other position or promotional opportunity that you'd like to explore. Find out what's required, what are the constraints and the requisites. Then visualize it, write about it, tell others about it, and make a plan to achieve it, using the process of climbing the Ts.

2. Ask for exploratory interviews, those that are for the purpose of getting acquainted, understanding mutual needs and aspirations. Get your name out there by doing at least one exploratory each month, if you are employed and two each week if you are unemployed. At the end of one year you should be able to look back and see that you've talked to several people who will instantly think of you for positions for which you have the appropriate attributes and experience.

3. Start looking for a mentor, someone that you admire and can look to for guidance and honest feedback.

EIGHT

FOR THE ENTREPRENEUR IN YOU

Rachel Gordon had been very happy at a TV station in the Rochester, New York, area as a sales professional on a 100 percent commission basis. She was accustomed to the highs and lows of the business and took it in stride. Because she didn't know how each pay period would turn out, she quickly learned to manage her income very efficiently, in a way that would pay dividends when she decided to become self-employed. Rachel learned to live within her means, paying with cash, or using her credit card for convenience but making sure she had the cash on hand.

As time wore on and the job became more demanding, Rachel decided she needed more balance between job and family and decided to do something about it (see chapter 10, "Mind, Body, and Spirit," on the importance of balance). She realized, after thirteen years in this position, that she did not love her job as before. Rachel came to the realization that she wanted to do something else. But she did not want to leave her sales position on a low note as this was not her nature. The thrill of closing a big deal was within reach and in her mind the best time to plan her exit. She closed a multi-hundred-thousand-dollar deal and then announced that it was time for her to explore other opportunities. Because of that, the management has expressed to her that she is always welcome back.

I doubt that Rachel will go back.

Rachel has been self-employed now for four years and has replaced the income she earned in sales. More importantly, she is fully in charge. She goes as fast or as slow as she wants, maintaining balance between her family's needs and her responsibilities to her clients. When she started out in her own business, her vision was simply to be the best advisor and consultant to her clients.

Rachel's goal has always been to help her clients grow and succeed—and get paid! She chose a deliberate growth pace, not too fast. Her style is to continue to do a good job and overdeliver, exceeding her clients' expectations.

Although Rachel did not start out with a business plan, she said she had "almost like an epiphany." She realized that losses in life are for a reason, and she felt very fortunate, very grateful for what she had with her family. But Rachel wanted something different, so she went out on her own. She has replaced her former salary and is doing it on her own terms. Rachel seeks the advice of others, particularly for legal and financial topics. She is wisely putting together a board of advisors (read more about boards of advisors later in this chapter) who will voluntarily help her with advice and counsel for her business. Rachel pays for some of the help she receives, or she barters for services.

"No regrets" is how Rachel views her current circumstances. "You can meet your paycheck and exceed it in a year or two with solid relationships and hard work." What if she were offered a job with a lucrative salary and package of benefits, would she go back? "Not unless I absolutely had to!" was her quick answer. "My husband supports my decision [to be self-employed] 110 percent." But she also adds that timing is everything—her husband has a job that has all the necessary health care benefits for her family, so their financial foundation is solid, in place. They are prudent, they think things through.

That's the key, planning your work, and working your plan.

Is Entrepreneurship for You?

Many try, but only some succeed in self-employment. Rachel's example above is a success story, but how many flower shops and restaurants and Web development small businesses failed during the same period that Rachel's business thrived?

My contention is that it's not enough to have a great idea. It's not enough to have the necessary personal attributes to succeed in self-employment. And it's not enough to have capital (I know of a generous man who purchased and capitalized a thriving business for his son-in—law, who then ran it into the ground in only eighteen months). Actually, it's those three: a clever idea, sufficient capital, and appropriate personal characteristics—attributes—that are minimally required. It also requires a "Blue Ocean" market of opportunity (see recommended reading: *Blue Ocean Strategy*) and time. Ramping up in self-employment takes *time*.

Wall Street Journal writer Kelly K. Spors wrote an excellent article about what it takes to be a successful entrepreneur. He said, "Building a successful business can take years filled with setbacks, long hours and little reward." Amen. I know about this personally (please read my story in chapter 6, "Comfort Zone

Disposition = Disastrous Consequences," about my own failed automotive and marine repair business.) One of the first requirements in starting a business or becoming self-employed is the ability to take significant financial risk. I personally know two high-profile entrepreneurs in our region who pledged their own homes and personal property to sustain their failing businesses. When they filed for bankruptcy, they lost it all. They each owed over $2.5 million to creditors. They had to sell everything they owned, including their furniture.

The purpose of this chapter is not to discourage you from entrepreneurship! It is to open your eyes and make sure that you prepare sufficiently to reduce the possibility of failure. In our nation, our culture, and our society, there is equal opportunity—but not equal results. This process of finding a business you can carry—creating it and sustaining it—is a lot more work than finding a job. Yes, *it's a lot more work than looking for a job.* That's why it's so important to make sure you have the necessary skills, knowledge, and attributes, plus capital.

Tips for Successful Entrepreneurship I

If you want to be successful in business, then you should be prepared as follows:

- Make sure you have the personality to embrace the many sacrifices that will surely accompany self-employment—long hours at little or no pay for months or years.
- This process works best if you have a significant other who is a "safety net"; if your partner has a steady income to cover your basic household expenses and health care benefits, *and is a willing partner in you new enterprise,* then you have a better chance in navigating the rough waters ahead, including possibly long stretches of time without net business income.
- Decide how much money you can lose and still be able to recover. Set a figure and stick to it, for example, six months without income, or one year or two.
- *Do not pledge your home,* or any family assets, to secure a business. Keep your retirement pay and home separate from your business. As mentioned above, I've seen two businessmen pledge their homes, and when their businesses failed, they both lost their house, their furniture, and subsequently their families. If pledging your house is the only way you can get started, then you're not ready to start.
- Entrepreneurship is a major lifestyle change. No more paid vacations. No paid sick days. No paid personal days. No mental health days. As a

business owner, you have to be at the beck and call of your customers. If you decide to start a retail business, like a convenience store, then get ready to be at work physically or mentally, 24-7 x 365 days a year. Is that what you want? I know a couple, husband and wife, who were both laid off by their employer on the same day. They saw this as an opportunity so they took their money and purchased a large bed-and-breakfast. Sounds idyllic, doesn't it? But running a B&B is a twenty-four-hour operation. For eight years they have not taken one day off. Not one. Eight years.

But there is success at the end of the tunnel. And for some, unparalleled success! Let's take a look at another successful entrepreneur, and see how she did it.

First, Get Fired!

Walking into the Van Bortel Subaru dealership showroom in Victor, New York, I hear a voice over the loudspeaker, "Sales call, pick up line 2!"

At the back of the forty feet by ninety feet clean, bright but modestly furnished showroom, Catherine "Kitty" Van Bortel picks up the phone: "Hi, may I help you?" She begins a conversation with a customer.

Kitty's desk is just like everyone else's in the showroom. She does not have a private office. What she does have is a clear view of every customer interaction in that room. As Kitty discusses features and prices with the customer on the phone, she consults her PC for spreadsheets and various lists of models and features. The conversation is very detailed; Kitty compares her Subaru products with other makes and models that the customer is considering. In a very informative way, she carries on this conversation while I wait, seated next to her, to interview her for this book.

Kitty uses her calculator and plugs numbers into an Excel spreadsheet on her PC to provide different payment scenarios to the customer on the phone. While looking up some facts, she turns to me and asks, "Are you a car salesman?" I reply, "No, actually, I'm a writer, an author, I'm here to interview you for my new book, but I do love cars!" She says, "I don't particularly like cars, except as a very useful device that helps people get things done and keeps them safe while doing so."

Oh.

With a high degree of concentration and sense of urgency, Kitty gets back on the phone with her customer and emphasizes the safety features and gas mileage of the Subaru products. She says enthusiastically to her customer, "Why don't you come over tonight and go for a test drive, the Legacy is a gorgeous car!" She ends the forty-minute discussion by saying to the customer, "When you come in, please ask for me, my name is Kitty."

The customer on the phone had no idea that he was talking directly to the president and CEO of America's highest volume Subaru dealer, which, when combined with Van Bortel Ford, constitutes a $125 million enterprise. That's Kitty's style. "I haven't changed." She says, meaning that she is still managing the customer interactions today as she did when she was selling used cars on her front lawn twenty years ago (today she sells over two hundred Subarus per month). Kitty literally doesn't lose sight of her customers; sitting in that open room, every time a phone rings her ear perks up, and if it rings three times she picks it up herself. But how did she start in this business?

"I was fired!" She said in a matter-of-fact way. "I was working for this dealer as sales manager for BMW and Mercedes, doing great. I had the highest numbers. Then they fired me after two years. They said they wanted to put some men on the sales team. I was devastated, shocked, and angry. But this event became my driving force. I wanted to show [that dealer] that I had what it takes."

When Kitty started out on her own, she had the support of her parents who were entrepreneurs. She realizes many young people don't have that support; they are lacking affirmation for starting a business. "Their parents are scared, they want their children to have the security of a paycheck. But I had the support of my parents." To get her business started after she was fired, Kitty sold her house, paid off everything she owed, and rented a house on a busy road in Victor, a suburb of Rochester, New York. She lived upstairs and sold used cars on the front lawn. "I started with $500. I bought a used car and sold it for six times that, so I was on my way."

When I asked her if she always had a vision for what she wanted as a business, she said, "I wanted all my people in the business to be professional, to dress with suits and ties, the women in dresses, stockings, high heels, to be like a Wall Street firm. But I thought I would do it with high-end used cars, like Porsches, Mercedes, and so on. I didn't envision a dealership like this." Everyone in her showroom is wearing suits, ties, dresses, stockings, and heels. "I also knew what I didn't want. Most dealers are all about the numbers, and they scare people, especially women. I wanted to treat my people very well, to hire women for the showroom and make the car purchasing experience as easy as possible, to take away the fear." At her dealership, the price of every car is 2 percent above invoice, "That way everyone pays the same price for the same kind of car. It's not right to charge different prices for the same car."

There are other Subaru dealers in the area, but Kitty wanted to differentiate herself. She listened to her mother's counsel: "My mother told me it's all about the reputation. It took me years to establish my reputation, and my reputation is everything. Many dealers are all about the numbers. My integrity and reputation are most important. What motivates me is not how many cars I can sell or how much money I can make. It's about how the car is reflective of the person owning it. I know I'm different—all the emotions about owning a car, that's what I address and work on every day—that's my niche."

As I was thinking of a question about how she runs her business on a daily basis, she reads my mind and says, "Everything in this dealership is delegated to very competent people except how to deal with the customer. I have good people in accounting, in marketing, in back-office operations. But the customer relationship, that I don't delegate. When someone comes in here [the showroom], I expect that they'll be greeted right away. I will do everything I can to make the [car purchasing] experience less stressful."

One example she names off the cuff: "I have this customer who has bought about ten cars from me over the years. His son wanted rear wing for his Subaru WRX [a high performance car]. So at Christmas I played Santa Claus, and I gave him a rear wing for his car. It was only $400 bucks to me, but their kid was thrilled, and they've been great customers."

When asked about mentors, Kitty responded that she has one person in particular that she relies on for advice: "We used to work together before I was fired. Now he's got his own very successful dealership."

How difficult was it getting started? "You have to have the capital, be properly capitalized. It took me five years before I could stop worrying about making payroll, having enough so I could pay my bills and not run out of cash. Every Sunday, for years, I would come in the office and count my cash and receivables to make sure I had enough to get through the week. It was scary, very hard work, very hard." One Sunday she realized she didn't have sufficient money. "After working on Sundays I used to have coffee with this friend in Fairport [New York]. But this one Sunday I knew I was done, it was over, I didn't have the cash I needed. I went to see my friend, sobbing, and told him about it. I told him that all this work for all these years and now I'm done, finished. He said, "No, you're not done." He went in the back of his place and came in with $50,000 in cash and said, "Here, just pay me back when you can." That was incredible! I would have never thought someone would do that. I had no idea he had that kind of money. I was meant to meet him. This may sound corny, but *it was spiritual*."

As our interview progressed, even though she has only known me for a few minutes, Kitty is open, genuine, accessible. She shares with me how she met her husband and started her family. Her sincerity is palpable. In the space of a one-hour interview, I have pages and pages of notes. Her caring, sensitive, and compassionate personality infuses the whole business.

Kitty doesn't forget the early years. "People don't realize how hard this is, to get started. People look at a successful business owner and say, "If he can do it, I can do it." But it's incredibly hard, incredibly hard getting started." I asked Kitty if she has any advice for would-be entrepreneurs: "The mistake people make is that if they become successful they change, they forget their roots, they become something else. But I haven't changed."

Kitty knows that it's important to have expertise on hand, so she has helpers in specialized areas, in accounting and finance, in banking, information technology and Web sites, in marketing, in social media, and a legal advisor. She has one friend in particular, whom she's known for forty-seven years, seated at the desk nearest to her.

Does Kitty have any regrets about being in business? "None."

Would Kitty accept an incredibly lucrative job offer to work for a company? "No."

Ironically, Kitty purchased the Subaru dealership from that same dealer who fired her in 1985. "He said that the brand was worthless, that he couldn't make any money from it." Only 3 percent of automobile dealerships are owned by women, and Subaru resisted Kitty's initiative; it took her one and one half years of badgering Subaru before they gave her the opportunity. She purchased the dealership in 1991 and immediately turned it into a top 20 agency. By 1996, her dealership had the highest volume in the nation. Kitty has been in the top 2 in the nation ever since.

Daily Grind—Multitasking

If you've been working in a large company, a Fortune 500 company, then you're well acquainted with job descriptions, territorial boundaries, and have probably said only half in jest, "That's not my job." or "That's above my pay grade." Those are organizations where thousands of tasks are distributed among thousands of people. But if you are contemplating self-employment, then you have to bear in mind that those same (seemingly) thousands of tasks can only be done by you.

Do you like cold calling?

Do you like invoicing?

Do you like writing follow-up correspondence?

Do you like taking phone calls from customers after 5:00 p.m. or before 8:00 a.m.?

Do you like creating and maintaining files? Photocopying?

Do you like debugging your personal computer? Changing ink cartridges in your printer?

Do you like designing your own marketing materials? Do you like marketing?

Are you comfortable networking and prospecting?

Do you like business development, e.g., selling?

Have you ever filed quarterly tax returns?

This list is endless. And you are the only employee in your start-up.

The question you must answer is, *is this who you are?* Can you solve problems every minute of the day with few or no resources? Are you psychologically and mentally equipped to face another day of unexpected issues, which can range from problems with service delivery, to product quality, to customer questions and even power outages during critical customer file downloads?

Nothing in your resume is likely to help you here. This is about resourcefulness and problem solving, minute by minute, all day long, working long hours, often by yourself and finding that you miss the camaraderie and informal talent pool of the water cooler.

- How well do you function without an overarching management structure? Successful entrepreneurs like making decisions. They thrive on the ambiguity of the situation, of the lack of clarity of every day, and then making something of it. Are you good at making plans and then executing those plans without supervision?
- How well do you execute on your own plans and action items? Do you leave everything until the last minute? If you fail to anticipate, or if you procrastinate, you will struggle being self-employed. Successful business owners are always thinking ahead, anticipating customer demand (or lack of it), understanding how technology can help/hurt their business model. They become familiar with competitors and their methods. This requires analysis and execution.

The decision to become self-employed places great emphasis on the word *self.*

But all great companies had a small starts. Let's look at another example of a successful entrepreneur.

I Feel Alive!

"Once you are an entrepreneur, you become unemployable." David Mammano's unhesitant response to my question speaks volumes about the drive and fervent ambition of an entrepreneur. I had asked him: "If someone offered you a job now, paying very well with good benefits in a well-established successful company, would you quit your business and take that job?" He was resolute in his refusal. He knew from a very young age that he wanted to have his own business, be independent, controlling standards of quality and company culture. "If it is your calling, you owe it to yourself to give it a shot," he exhorts young and old.

Sitting in his corner office on the second floor of a historically significant brick building in the "four corners" area of Victor, New York, David discusses how he found a service gap for high school students, created a magazine to address it, and now manages a $3 million enterprise. David Mammano is founder and CEO of Next Step Publishing, Inc., which includes a glossy, high-quality magazine distributed five times a year to 20,500 high schools in the United States.

Years ago, David had been selling radio advertising, but he was not excited about it. He felt he had so much more to offer, and although he liked his boss, he hated having a boss! David wanted to do his own thing from a very young age: "I wanted to create something from scratch." To him, being in business looked very exciting because he would be able to control the quality of his products and services. His vision for a business came as he realized that a resource was needed for high school students considering college. As he interviewed and asked college-bound students, as well as students already in college, why they were choosing those colleges and those courses of study, he recognized that they were lost, they were not adequately informed. They were making costly mistakes for themselves and their parents, who were paying tuition, room, and board. David asked, "What if there was a resource for high school students?" He then shaped and formed his concept for what came to be *Next Step Magazine*; this was done to create an objective, neutral resource for high school students so they could think about and understand why they were continuing their education in college. There are many articles in the magazine—preparing for SAT exams, financial aid, types of colleges and their advantages and disadvantages—these are data that students need in order to make thoughtful decisions.

Aren't there other informational resources for high school students? David explains, "The unique value proposition of *Next Step* is that it provides the best, most objective content in the business for college-bound students. We have the widest reach, with over 20,500 high schools distributing our magazines in seventeen regional editions. We are not selling, we are providing top quality content." Just by picking up a copy of his latest edition, his words become tangible in my hands.

I asked him, "David, did you seek the advice of others? What types of people did you approach?" David got his start when he was twenty-five. He asked local Paychex, Inc., founder and billionaire, Tom Golisano, for a lunch meeting, and Tom accepted. They had lunch at the Northside Inn, a hangout for business people in East Rochester, New York. David explained his idea for a magazine at that time, and he remembers that Mr. Golisano did not like the idea because he thought David was going to sell subscriptions. But once David explained more that the magazine was free in bulk to the high schools and that revenue would come from advertising, then he changed his tune. Mr. Golisano paid for their lunch, David remembers. More recently, David asked Mr. Golisano for lunch at upscale Biaggi's, and this time David was quite proud to pay for lunch. David has also sought the wisdom and experience of other serial entrepreneurs, like Dick Kaplan, CEO of Pictometry International Corporation, and Arunas Chesonis, CEO of PAETEC Corporation.

David's confessions that at one point his business grew so fast that it got out of control, "I hit the wall." He then realized that he needed to assemble his leadership team in such a way as to optimize their individual talents, which is another way of saying that he had to allow them to check his impulses. Once he gave them sufficient authority to stand up to him, it smoothed out some of his "all engines at full speed" inclination. David loves to watch his people grow, and he has encouraged his team to balance work and personal life. David leaves the office at 5:30 p.m. every evening to have supper with his wife and two children.

David advises, "If this is your calling [to be an entrepreneur], you owe it to yourself to give it a shot." He started Next Step in 1995, in Rochester, New York, and distributed the magazine to fifty high schools. By the third issue, he had positive cash flow and expanded to Syracuse and Buffalo, New York. In 1997, his magazine was in every high school in New York, and by 2005 in the entire nation, with franchisees in seventeen regions.

David quotes Anthony Robbins, "If you're committed, you'll always find a way."

Growing Pains

You don't make people responsible, you hire responsible people. You don't make people accountable, you hire accountable people.
—Cameron Herold

If you start a business in, say, Web site development, you're probably doing so precisely because you are good at it—you have a knack, a talent so your product or service is elegant and desirable. Your graphic designs and elegant architecture are showing up at important client Web sites. As your client list expands, you find yourself needing a helper. That's great! Success!

If you only want to work on that specific skill set you used to launch your business, then you'll either have to turn down work or take on helpers. But let's say that orders are coming in and you decide to grow; you put the word out to your network that you need an assistant. You interview several people and decide to hire a bright young lady with all the requisite skills for your business line.

Your new helper comes on board and now you have everything you used to do plus looking after your assistant. You then discover that you are an early morning person and want to be productive by 8:00 a.m., but she hates getting up early, so she's frequently late for work and cranky when she does show up. Adjustments are made in your fledgling company's operations to accommodate different lifestyles. You find very quickly that some of your time that you used to spend directly on what you love to do is now channeled to coordinate and manage the processes and outputs of your new assistant. In addition to her preference for working five hours later than you, she has a "global," big picture view of things and is not concerned about trivial things like spelling, syntax, on even tact for customers. You hired her because of her thousands of followers in Twitter and her knack and appetite for the latest application for mobile media. But you just can't see eye to eye with her. The two of you are very different. This professional relationship should have worked, but you're further behind, and you're paying her a salary!

What went wrong?

Tips for Successful Entrepreneurship II

Let's continue to build on a list of tips and tactics for successful self-employment, particularly as you gain momentum and begin to grow:

- When you take on staff and employees, a great deal of your mindshare will be devoted to coordinating and managing their work, their methods, their quality, and their interactions with customers. You'll come home after a stressful day saying, "I would love my work, if it wasn't for these people [your employees]." The solution? Very, very careful attention to your hiring process.
- In your hiring process, make sure you understand not just what that person knows—their skills and talents—but what they are like as individuals. Ask them about their likes and dislikes, how they function every day, their ways and means of getting things done. Ask them if they do their best work early in the morning or very late in the evening.
- It is easiest for you to identify the skills of a candidate, as it relates to what you do in your business, because that's precisely what you know best. But especially in a very small work environment where everyone has to pitch in and help in many different ways, you should be most concerned about their attributes. You can teach them the technical aspects, but you won't be able to change who they are.
- Take the time to know them. All the time you spend upfront, getting to know them, is well worth it. And this is not about technical

expertise—that should be a given—you would not be interviewing someone who does not have or cannot learn the technical aspects of the work. This is about understanding who they are and whether the two of you are compatible.

- Do not hire people "who look like you," meaning that they behave just as you do. There has to be compatible diversity in your work styles. For example, in the hypothetical situation noted above, with the assistant who liked working late at night and hated waking up early, use her work habits to take care of customers calling in late in the day from the West Coast or from the Pacific Rim. She can do all this while you are at home having dinner and enjoying your family. She can leave you a report late at night, which you can read in the morning and then give her further direction.

- Being self-employed requires self-structure. As I discuss growing pains with other entrepreneurs, one thing in common among them is the sense of a lack of a structure. To be your own boss means you have to be very self-disciplined. Your daily/weekly/monthly calendar must be filled with productive activity. Not just activity—productive, meaningful activity. One of the coaching tools that I use with my clients who are looking for a job (which is a form of self-employment) is to ask to see their weekly calendar. They are then embarrassed because they (a) don't have any plans, their calendar is bare, or (b) the weekly calendar is filled with pro bono work at many not-for-profits. Your calendar, of which you are the master, must have a balanced amount of *productive activity*, meaning activity which is likely to yield results, preferably monetary results. Your calendar must also be balanced and have time for family, mind, body, and spirit (see chapter 10, "Mind, Body, and Spirit").

If your business begins to grow, then you'll begin to think about the sort of people you need for assistance with your growth; people who are compatible with your way of thinking, with the way you view the business world, with your values (what I call your *business religion*), and the way you get things done.

Board of Advisors

If you want to receive great advice at no cost, then build a board of advisors. A board of advisors (BOA) is a small group of three to five people, whom you know and trust. They are each experts in their own field, and they have admirable business acumen and personal attributes. Look over your Rolodex of contacts and select a list of candidates. Then ask to meet with them individually, interview them (yes, interview them), tell them what you have in mind—that you want to gather a short list of people whom you can call and ask for business advice from time to time.

I've done this, and in fact, I have three boards of advisors: one for book writing and publishing made up of five published authors. Another one for my life and career coaching enterprise called Gran Altura, Inc., and also for my strategic management consulting firm called Human Capital Strategy Partners. Then I have a third board for a not-for-profit 501c(3) memorial foundation.

My BOA members all know each other; they know why they've been selected, and they are filled with a sense of purpose in helping me with my business growth. In business life, I can't think of a more rewarding relationship than being asked to join or asking others to join a board of advisors. In fact, I have developed this concept to the point that I am actually a consultant to companies who lack a BOA, helping them with the strategy and process of setting one up. If you're curious, my BOA members are named in the acknowledgments.

I think it's critically important to have sound advice as you embark on this path of self-employment. And what easier way to do it than to ask those who have succeeded to help you? You might ask, "Why would anyone help me for free?" Because there are many, many people who, when they become successful, now have a burning desire to help others. Their only request is that you would actually implement their suggestions from time to time. If you meet with them and ask for their help but continue doing the same thing (and getting the same poor results), it's understandable that they would lose interest in helping you. But if you apply their advice and obtain better business results, they will be as proud of you as you are of your work.

Tips for Successful Entrepreneurship III

Continuing to identify some important stepping stones on a pathway to successful entrepreneurship:

- Successful entrepreneurs are good salespeople, not only for their products and services, but even more importantly for their vision for their business. While any business can hire and retain successful sales professionals, it's the business owner who has to have an infectious confidence about their business idea. If you are considering being self-employed, can you clearly and convincingly articulate your idea and business model? Can you be a proselytizer, an advocate for your business case?

- If you have a business idea in mind, then ask yourself why you would start that particular business. What are you after? Independence? Money? Prestige? Lifestyle? The word *passionate* has become very popular since I published the first edition of this book, but the question is apropos: are you passionate about dry cleaning services? Do you have a passion for writing applications for mobile devices? Does a tanning salon stir your soul? Sounds trite. It's not. You, more than anyone, must understand why you want to start a business, and the type of business it is, and how it will be different from all that went before. By the way, how did Ray Krock differentiate MacDonald's hamburgers from its competitors at the inception of what became the world's largest restaurant chain? Did he do it with the Big Mac? Or with Chicken McNuggets? Neither. He did it with clean restrooms.

- How resilient are you? Successful entrepreneurs will regale you with stories of how they were down and out but then came back and made it. Some came back from the business dead more than once. Some "serial entrepreneurs" have had their hand at several businesses, only some of which survived, and maybe only one of which actually made much money. You have to be ready for many discouraging turns of events, many disappointments; you have to be resilient in the face of sometimes fierce opposition to your business.

- Can you go it alone? Or do things go better with a business partner? This is a not insignificant consideration and pause point. While a business partner can add very significant value to a young enterprise, the relationship has to be as good as a marriage, if it's to last. For example, if you have a great, patented invention, you may want to stay back in the lab and let others handle the operations and sales. Or if you are a finance expert, you may want to find a great idea person, where your value add is searching for and locating startup capital. Understanding the need for a partner is only the beginning. The real work is finding a compatible partner.

A Few More Ideas

Sometimes a businessman is not what s/he appears to be. I have a client who functions as the operations chief of a multinational information technology company. He goes about his business quietly, unobtrusively, even humbly. Many of my colleagues know about this business and about its president and chief executive officer (not my client); they are eager to arrange meetings with the CEO. But what my colleagues don't know is that my client, the COO, is in fact the majority owner of the company and the chairman of the board. The point is that my client, who founded the company and ran it for many years, eventually had enough sense to step aside and hire someone else to be the CEO under his direction, someone who has skills, experience, and attributes that he lacks. Wise decision.

Also, think of alternative avenues. Sometimes the sources of wealth of a business owner are not what they seem. I have a friend who owns a very successful software applications development firm with 150 employees. He loves designing and selling software apps. But all the money that supports his well-to-do lifestyle comes not from the software company, but from an old hobby he's had since college—collecting and trading gold jewelry. Earnings from the software company are plowed right back into its growth. But the profits from trading gold jewelry are what support a comfortable lifestyle for his family.

Still Want to Be an Entrepreneur?

Look, I tried it once, I failed, I lost a lot of money, I learned a lot and now I'm doing it again. The answer is not always clear, the pathway to entrepreneurial success is not always well lit, but these are a few major lessons that I learned:

- *Some enterprises are capital intensive*: raising capital is the first major obstacle of an entrepreneur, and it requires teamwork and connections. In my case, I didn't realize how much capital was needed just to run a repair facility for high-end cars and racing boats. The customers were there, our skills and connections were sufficient, but we needed at least two years of cash flow and capital for tools, technology, and overhead to keep us going, especially through winter months, but we weren't prepared.
- *Find a business with little capital requirements*: during the significant economic downturn of 2008-2009, many thousands of executives and subject matter experts lost their jobs. Many of them became consultants. Overnight there were legions of consultants knocking on doors of surviving businesses. Consulting has very low capital requirements. All you need is a cell phone, laptop PC, and some business cards and you're in business. This wave of consultants created a "red ocean" of competitors. Lesson learned: identify your "blue ocean" opportunity very quickly, and create your brand in that market for first-mover advantage (required reading: *Blue Ocean Strategy* by W. Chan Kim and Renée Mauborgne).
- *Go national as quickly as possible*: what's the old saying "You can't be a prophet in your own land"? Unless you are performing a very

personalized service, like massage therapy, or opening a bistro, you need to establish a brand elsewhere, and then bring it back home. For example, my blue ocean opportunity market for life and career coaching is highly educated, highly intelligent people (like you!). At the very center of my target audience are highly intelligent, highly educated Hispanics. This is so *porque todo lo que hago en inglés lo puedo hacer igualmente en español* (because everything I do in English I can do equally well in Spanish), so that's my natural audience. While there are thousands of Hispanic executives in my community, there are millions globally. That's my sweet spot—the entire global Hispanic executive community. How do I reach them? To reach them, I uncovered many professional associations of Hispanics. I asked if I could be a speaker at the national and regional conferences, I wrote articles for them, I conducted workshops, and I even opened an office in Miami, Florida, which has many thousands of Hispanic executives. And it worked! Now, having done many national-level speaking engagements, my stock is much higher in my home community.

- *Above all, anticipate, anticipate, anticipate*: Whatever you are doing now, it will change. Your audience will drift away, technology will interfere, your business model/product/service may become obsolete (remember VHS videotapes and players?). Use evolving technology to your advantage. Meet with your audience/market and ask them what they're thinking. Connect with forward-thinking entrepreneurs and see how they move at the race track, how they navigate through traffic to lead the race and to win.

- *Ask for help*: there are many, many successful entrepreneurs who are willing to help a sincere, hardworking aspiring business person—like you! Successful entrepreneurs are by their very nature social beings. They like being around people, getting things done through people. If you approach them and offer to buy them breakfast, bring a list of questions about a business you are considering; they will sit with you and offer you their wisdom. Sure, you can find a noncooperative business owner from time to time, but don't be discouraged. The cooperative, helpful, well-connected successful entrepreneurs willing to help you will vastly outnumber the curmudgeons. So ask for help.

Companies that nurture flexibility, awareness, and resiliency are more likely to survive the crisis, and even to prosper.
—Lowell Bryan and Diana Farrell, McKinsey & Co.

One Final Thought: On Giving

If you've read this chapter to conclusion, it's probably because you have more than a passing interest in self-employment, in or sharpening your business toolkit. I'll leave you with this thought as you start or continue your pathway to entrepreneurial success.

In your business, what are you giving away—with no expectation of return? What part of your value or of your services are you rendering to others as your gift for the **greater good**? And you may be asking, why this topic now? Well, if you suspect that this topic was chosen to set you up to make a philanthropic donation to a worthy cause, you are right! It's about your cause. This is a business topic—about your business.

> *For it is in giving that we receive*
> —St. Francis of Assisi

We establish our businesses to earn an income, to be economically self-sufficient, to be productive for ourselves and others. That is understood. But there is room in that profit motive equation for charity, not just the traditional type of charity of benevolent donations to worthy causes, but charity with an intent of benefiting the greater good, of which we are also a part. Sounds circuitous, doesn't it? Let me use two specific examples to illustrate, one of a local entrepreneur, the second one of a national magazine.

My friend Scott owns a bicycle shop in my neighborhood. I'm an avid cyclist, and some years ago when I needed a new pair of cycling shoes I went through several catalogues and found exactly what I wanted. The shoes were identically priced at $179.99 in three catalogs. I took all three catalogs to Scott and said to him, "These are the shoes I want. Please order them from your sources and I'll pay you the catalog price, so you can have the profit." He ordered the shoes, and a few days later he called me to come pick them up. When I came to get the shoes he charged me $120. I said, "Scott, you're giving me a big break here, sixty dollars . . ." He said, "No worries, I made my money." Well, can you guess what I've been doing ever since? He gave me a $60 savings that I wasn't expecting so ever since then I've been buying every article for bicycling from him and singing his praises! How many customers have I sent his way who have bought his high-end bikes? He gave of himself, expecting nothing—we didn't have an agreement, not even implicitly, for a price break. But in doing so he gained a great deal more. (Visit Scott Likly, Towpath Bicycles, Pittsford, New York)

The second example is **Fast Company** magazine. When it was launched, they held to a principle of sharing and giving their information, the content of their articles, freely and openly. Now, more than a decade later I love to receive my copy of *Fast Company* in the mail for its contemporary and timely content. But wait, there's more. I also love to go on their Web site and search their archives for topics of interest: on leadership, on entrepreneurship, on branding (personal and corporate), on social media—the list is endless. Don't try that at home with other publications. *Fast Company* archives are easy to find—and they are free. Many other publications, including our city newspaper, charge at least ten bucks for an archived article. At *Fast Company* they have adhered to a spirit of giving, a spirit that others need to emulate. Look at the evidence: in this part of my book I've just told you about two enterprises that keep on giving.

Is your brand known for giving?

Summary

Entrepreneurship is the heart of our business culture. It's very strong in this era of a deep recession simply because millions of highly intelligent, highly educated people have been without a job for months, so they have used their intellectual and financial capital to start small businesses. But it's an arduous task at best and highly stressful quite often.

The success stories are the ones we see in magazines and articles. We can learn from those who are successful, if we have their temperament and sufficient capital to last through very difficult early months and years.

A board of advisors is highly recommended, as even the most intelligent and experienced will eventually need help in navigating many difficult circumstances on their pathway to entrepreneurial success.

Homework

1. If you have sufficient capital and a desire to start a business, go to a group like SCORE in your community. They are there to help small businesses get started. Ask them how to get started with a business plan. They are very experienced, and there is no cost or obligation.
2. If you are proceeding in this direction, make sure you discuss this with your significant other. There will be a lot of sleepless nights, and you'd want all the emotional support you can get.
3. An excellent source of support will be a board of advisors. Make sure you put one together; all you need is three to five people with specialized knowledge or skills.

Nine

THE NEW WORLD—SOCIAL MEDIA

Linked In? Or Left Out?

One phenomenon that has grown exponentially since the first edition of this book is networking using social media, also referred to as Web 2.0 (web-two-point-o). While young college students and recent graduates are very familiar with Facebook, Twitter, and MySpace media for social networking, more experienced professionals and business-only networkers appreciate the power of business networking tools like LinkedIn.

LinkedIn has grown rapidly in recent years. When I joined LinkedIn in 2004, I often had to explain what it was to my business peers and friends; I had to show them why I found it valuable. Interestingly, many of my peers inside and outside Xerox at the time thought that networking tools like LinkedIn were a distraction. They didn't see the value, particularly since they were comfortable in their jobs, and perceived networking as something to do only if you became unemployed. But years ago I was using it as a very effective (and free) networking research tool. For example, if I wanted to look up the chief human resources officer (CHRO) of a specific company, I could use the Search tool in LinkedIn to find exactly that individual. Since a significant part of my job was to find and establish business relationships with thought leaders in human resources all over the nation on behalf of Xerox, I found LinkedIn to be an invaluable tool because it cuts across geographical and organizational boundaries. Over time, I was even able to persuade many of our internal recruiters that they could search for and approach "passive" candidates (those who were employed and not actively looking for work) who were leaders in their field. By approaching passive candidates, they could comb organizations for their best talent and inform them about our value proposition.

That was five years ago.

Today, LinkedIn is recognized as the single most often used vehicle in job search for professionals, and the most reliable and economical tool in any recruiter's toolbox.

Ironically, many of the people who often ignored my invitations to join my list on LinkedIn—while they were comfortably employed—have changed their minds and are now ever so eager to invite me to their lists because they became unemployed during the financial crisis of 2008-2009. They could have been networking while they were still employed, but they waited until they had a pink slip before they reluctantly accepted networking as a necessary part of life.

If you are employed and want to meet influential people who can assist you with your career, or if you are unemployed and looking for a job, then you can use business networking tools like LinkedIn to conduct searches of people in certain companies or industries or just to track down persons in our work history who may hold the key to a potential opportunity for introduction or advancement.

I encourage you to find out how social networking tools like LinkedIn work. LinkedIn is free for you and me. Just fill out your profile and reach out to people you know. Nowadays, all recruiters realize its value, and some of them pay a fee to take advantage of its powerful search, job posting, and advanced networking capabilities. In order for you to be "found," you have to go to where the recruiters go—LinkedIn.

Why Use Social Media?

My own social media advisor, Kelly Mullaney, explains the value of these social media tools and suggests how you can deploy them in your job search or in promoting your business brand. Here's Kelly's contribution:

What is Social Media?

By Kelly Mullaney, bilingual-bicultural social media expert

Social Media is about people connecting with other people. Twitter, Facebook, LinkedIn, they are all just tools at the end, each one effective at different levels. How you use them is what is going to determine if you really make the connection with that other person. When you sit in front of the computer, or your favorite device, don't forget that at the other end of the line there is another human being.

Social Media is great for networking, but not just to broadcast what you want to say; you'll need to do some listening, too. Interact and acknowledge those other people you want to connect with. They have the choice to respond back, and when they do, that's when it becomes a conversation. Otherwise it's as if you are standing alone in the middle of a room full of people, talking by yourself.

The way you present yourself and what you talk about in your Social Media network will determine whom you will attract. Even those little comments here and there, as a collective, are defining how people see you; they are building your brand.

Be genuine, because your true self always comes out, eventually. But also mind what you say and post online. You may think because you only have a handful of friends or followers or fans, your comments will not go too far, but you may not be able to take those words back.

You get what you put in. Be generous, share your knowledge, help others. People will appreciate what you do for them and will want to reciprocate. Some will want to stick around you, interested in what you have to say and what you have to offer. The more value you give the easier you can build a quality community on-line. You can surround yourself with people who share your interests, your vision. And that's the idea, right?

Kelly Mullaney at: Working Art Media
http://www.WorkingArtMedia.com

Who Is Your Audience?

If you want to invest some of your valuable time in social media, then the most important question you must answer is, Who is your audience? To whom will you be addressing your Tweets (comments on Twitter)? Who do you want following you on Twitter? Why? Whom will you follow? Why? To what end are you writing those comments and displaying those photos on Facebook? Who will you ask to join your LinkedIn list? Why? What's in it for you? What's in it for them?

If you don't know who your audience is, then you'll be trying to speak to the whole world, which is a hugely fruitless effort. I believe that discernment is necessary—cull out your target audience, address your messages to that audience, and thereby persuade your audience to *advocate for you!* This is often lost on those who just want to gather thousands of followers. I'm not impressed by sheer numbers and volume. My approach is different—I don't need many thousands, I only need the ones with whom I can have a relationship of mutual and reciprocal business (or social) benefit. Then I can advocate for them, and they can advocate for me.

The reason for using social media, or at least my reason for using social media, is mutual and reciprocal benefit—I can advocate for my followers, and they can advocate for me. For example, I began to follow a real estate agent in Coral Gables, Florida. Her name is Janie Coffey. My initial interest in following Janie was that my family owns a house in Coral Gables, a beautiful neighborhood in Miami. Janie knows a lot about real estate in Miami and particularly in Coral Gables. That was months ago. Fast-forward to today. Over time, Janie and I have established a good working relationship on Twitter. She knows what I do, and I understand her business interests. When I visit Miami, I visit her office and advocate for Janie, for her real estate business and her community history project (www.TheMiamiStory.com) whenever I can. She in turns gives me, through her followers, a voice in Miami, which is at the epicenter of my blue ocean market—Hispanic executives (see chapter 8, "For the Entrepreneur in You").

I can't emphasize enough that you need to (a) know your brand and (b) you need to identify your audience in social media. If you fail at either, you will have no results, or worse, confuse your audience to the point that they will not follow you at all or malign your name and brand.

ROI

You've heard in business that there has to be a return on investment, an ROI, for all capital invested in business. ROI is often measured as payback period. For example, a business invests in better heating/ventilation/air conditioning systems to reduce cost of utilities. In this example, let's say the payback period is calculated to be twenty-four months, e.g., the savings in monthly utility bills from the HVAC improvement will add up in just twenty-four months to offset the investment in upgraded equipment. That's referred to as a twenty-four-month payback.

Among the skeptics of social media, the question often arises—what is the ROI of social media? Let's accept the challenge—to understand and be able to demonstrate the ROI of social media. But to establish some ground rules, let's move the clock back to a simpler era, about twenty years ago, the "phone and fax" era, when the major means of communication were simply the telephone and fax machines. Now I'll ask you this question: in a large, multinational company in the year 1990, what was the ROI of hundreds of thousands of dollars paid out every month for long distance calls and fax transmissions? What was the company getting monetarily in return for its significant expense in telecommunications?

Let's make this even easier—what is the ROI of your landline telephone at your home? You have been using a telephone at home for decades. You have been paying a monthly invoice for many years. What have you received in return for the many thousands of dollars you have paid to your regional telephone company?

The answer: information.

Okay, we have our answer.

Now let's examine ROI of social media.

> *What is your ROI—return on ignorance—of social media?*
> —Jeffrey Hayzlett, Chief Marketing Officer, Eastman Kodak Co.

I've noticed that some people behave as if social media should go away, or they hope that it will go away as soon as everyone gets tired of updating their Facebook, MySpace, or Twitter accounts.

But social media is not going away. In fact, it's not only growing exponentially, it will inexorably continue to grow and technologically spawn other ways and means. Not so long ago Twitter didn't exist. And not so long ago, Facebook was strictly a social medium for college students. Some other media will rise up and eventually take their place (as Facebook is gradually replacing MySpace). But social media are here and can't be ignored.

e-Patients

Social media has even entered inside the tent of that innermost sanctum—the patient/physician relationship. In a lengthy, thought-provoking article by Thomas Ferguson, MD, we learn that "physicians can no longer go it alone." There is so much new information being published; they need the help of their well-informed patients. "Well-informed patients can help lift the burden of care from the shoulders of overworked clinicians." This is simply because the amount of information merging onto the medical mainstream is absolutely impossible for any one person to absorb. Enter the very focused, very well-informed patient. This e-patient has devoted countless hours researching his/her condition on the Internet. But there's more—the e-patient has joined a cyber network via social media, which has made all information about their condition available—free of charge. Now the e-patient makes an appointment with their family physician who may not be familiar with this rare condition. Dr. Ferguson explains, "Understanding this development on an intellectual level is one thing. But as many of us [physicians] can assure you, it is quite another to sit face-to-face with a patient newly diagnosed with a rare condition who has already spent countless hours reading up on it—while you can only dimly remember reading about it in medical school many years before." In fact, the river of information about medicine alone is incomprehensible. "If I read and memorized two medical journal articles every night, by the end of a year I'd be 400 years behind," according to Donald Lindberg, director of the National Library of Medicine.

The e-patient phenomenon spreads beyond physical ailments—to mental health therapy. People with mental health concerns have been looking for help via the Web for many years. Psychologist John Grohol, PsyD, coined the term *e-therapy* in 1993. He says, "From a public health point of view, e-therapy offers a way to reach millions of patients with psychological and mental health conditions who would be unlikely to seek face-to-face therapy." He does not suggest that it can or should replace traditional psychotherapy, "but it can provide people with an introduction to the benefits of the therapeutic relationship and process. It can be a stepping stone to regular therapy."

Think

Think: can you afford to ignore this social media phenomenon and continue to function as an informed observer, as a relevant participant in a business conversation, on any level, at any organization?

Back to the question, what do you gain by ignoring social media? What precisely is your *return on ignorance* of the profound effect of social media and its messages?

What to do? That's a fair question. You don't have to become a social butterfly on social media. That's not my point. In fact, that would be a waste of your time.

If you don't know what to do about social media, then try these simple steps:

1. *Understand your reason for using social media:* If you are self-employed, or you own a business of any kind, it makes a lot of sense for you to use social media to promote your products and services. You will be using social media to promote your business or yourself (when unemployed or wanting to change jobs). But you must know why you are spending time on social media channels. (See above "Who Is Your Audience?"). You will not be using social media to tell the world what you had for breakfast. You will instead be advocating for your business, for your products and services, or for yourself as a candidate for employment.

2. *Open a LinkedIn account:* If you are looking for work, you must open a LinkedIn account. After you revise your resume (see chapter 2 "Career Coaching 102: The Tool Kit"), open a LinkedIn account and fill out all the appropriate sections to complete your LinkedIn profile. This is a must. Everyone, and I mean everyone in business, is using LinkedIn. Read section above, "Linked In or Left Out?" Don't think about it anymore. Get on LinkedIn. Just do it.

3. *Open a Web site, or open a Facebook account* for business purposes which can be used as a free Web site: If you can afford to pay a few hundred dollars for a Web site, you will need at least a landing page, which you can update from time to time. Your objective is to create a platform that serves two purposes—one, a permanent place to lay out your value proposition in a personal way, including your photo or logo for your company, and two, to let others see who you are.

You can enter the world of social media and take advantage of all its benefits for free. Once you've paid for your computer, mobile phone, and connection services—the use of social media is totally free.

All A-Twitter

You have to read Twitter, if your job is to be up to date.
—Norma Holland, TV Journalist, News Anchor,
WHAM TV 13 Rochester, New York

Go to Twitter.com and open an account. You are not opening this account for you to post what you had for lunch. This is for you to follow important news and thought leaders in your field(s) of interest. At first, follow only those you know. You don't have to follow everyone. In fact, you should be discerning about whom you follow on Twitter. While you may get many requests to follow others, be discerning as you normally would be with friends, and follow those people who are interesting, inspiring, informational, who can help you with what you want to accomplish professionally, and with whom you can reciprocate.

After you open your Twitter account, using your real name and providing some tidbit about who you are, professionally, then follow news sources that you enjoy, such as National Public Radio, *The Wall Street Journal*, BBC News, Democratic National Committee, Republican National Committee, National Geographic, Food Network, Home and Garden, whatever. Find and follow those people who are at the top of their game in your field of interest or endeavor. You should know what they're saying.

Look, this is the ROI you're looking for—*up-to-the-minute information about those things for which you care deeply!*
Let's approach Twitter in stages:

1. *At first, you don't have to post anything in your Twitter account.* You don't have to say anything on Twitter. You can use your Twitter account strictly as an observer, just reading what other interesting people are saying. They will know you are following them, but you don't have to say anything. You can be perfectly quiet. It's as if you are watching a sports car race on your TV. You know what's going on but you are hundreds, even thousands of miles away, and you are not adding anything to the event. You are simply enjoying and using the information.

2. *Now get ready to write something:* Let's say that now you have something to say—something that you think will be of interest people in your audience who are by now following you. You can start by replying or direct messaging someone who wrote something that you found extraordinarily good. Thank them for their Tweet, and briefly tell them how much you enjoyed what they posted. As you become braver about all this, you can re-Tweet something interesting that someone said. Keep in mind that *replying and re-Tweeting are adding to your brand!* You are aligning yourself with what the other person is saying, that's why you have to be discerning—because it's adding to, or subtracting from—your brand.

3. *Create your own value add:* Write some original thoughts, make some observations of the world around you, but before you hit the Send button, think: how does this add to my brand? How is another person reading this, are they likely to react as I did? Am I going to be proud of this posting a year from now? Five years from now?

4. *Use Twitter to send potential clients/employers to your Web site or Facebook account:* Once you are comfortable with stage 3, you can easily coax your readers to visit your Web site or your Facebook account, where you have more information that would be of interest to them. Think of Twitter as the cyber invitation that you send to your audience to come take a closer look at you—in your Facebook or Web site.

5. *When you have something nice to say, say it on Twitter:* Look, we are all human, and we all love to see our name associated with something good. When someone does something you like, talk about it on Twitter, mention their name, or their company. Make that person feel good. Why? Because it's the right thing to do.

All social media activity, including Tweets, profile changes on LinkedIn, blogs, and updates comprise a significant component of your electronic footprint. These activities allow you, as a job seeker, the opportunity to construct and/or improve your online profile, keeping in mind that prospective employers are likely to research you online.

E-Mail or Hard Copy?

Electronic mail has virtually totally replaced hard copy as the medium for communication among employers and job candidates. But the perceived anonymity and informality of the e-mail medium can lead one astray. It's important to keep some principles in mind:

- With the first message to a target employer, or even to a networking contact, you should establish a sense of respect and formality. For example, don't begin your e-mail to a hiring manager by saying hi; address her/him formally, as "Dear Mr." or "Dear Ms.", or even "Dear Dr."

- Your cover letter can be included in the body of the e-mail, although preferably as an attachment in standard, updated software like Microsoft Word. But be cognizant that increasingly, some hiring managers may be using personal computing devices like the Blackberry, Treo, Droid, or iPhone devices, which may not be able to open attachments easily.

- Your resume can likewise be an attachment in MS Word, although you have to check to make sure that the recipient is able to open the attachment.

- Make sure your signature does not have cute or religious or pontificating sign-offs at the bottom of your e-mail. No one is amused by your attempt at humor or at proselytizing for politics or religion or even for dietary supplements.

Chapter Summary

The phenomenon of social media has interesting twists and turns. As I wrote this manuscript early one morning, I was keeping an eye on a regional TV news show. One of the news anchor personalities wrote a post on her Facebook account—while she was still on set during a break in the news show. I happened to see it and responded to her in Facebook. She replied, and we had a brief conversation on Facebook. She asked me to meet her for lunch the following week, and we settled on date, time, and place via Facebook—all the while she was doing the news on television. By the way, between her Facebook followers and mine, there were hundreds of people who could potentially read our Facebook conversation, but that's not important to us since what we were doing—setting a business lunch date—was not wrong or inappropriate.

Some people post some very immature and irrelevant comments on social media, but not all social media messages are silly and narcissistic. As I write this manuscript, the main source of information about a very serious political opposition movement and government repression in the nation of Iran is text information and photos taken with mobile devices (cell phones) and posted on Web sites and blogs around the world. The oppressed people of Iran know that truly (unlike at the Democratic National Convention in Chicago in 1968)—*the whole world is watching.*

The heaviest users of Web 2.0 applications are also enjoying benefits such as increased knowledge sharing and more effective marketing. These benefits often have a measurable effect on the business.
—McKinsey & Company, McKinsey Quarterly

Homework

1. Do you have a LinkedIn account? If not, put this book down and spend an hour creating a profile and inviting about a dozen other professionals.
2. If you do have a LinkedIn account, when was the last time you updated it? How many people are waiting for you to respond to their invitations?
3. Do you know some basics about Facebook? About Twitter? About Web sites for professional purposes? Answers to many basic questions can be easily found in Wikipedia.com. Wiki means quickly, as in quick encyclopedia. Wikipedia is a search engine like Google, and it's quite reliable. Find many social media answers in this social media

tool—Wikipedia. (Please note that Wikipedia is not always accurate as users can and do update it frequently without validation. It's a great source of information, but like much of what's available through the Internet, the content should be only be considered with healthy skepticism or independent verification.)

TEN

MIND, BODY, AND SPIRIT

On the Importance of Being Balanced

And in the end it's not the years in your life that count.
It's the life in your years.
—Abraham Lincoln

Think of a tall pyramid. A tall pyramid has a broad base, and the broader its base, the higher its summit. Now think about a pyramid upside down. It's totally unstable. It can tilt at any moment in any direction, resulting in damage or destruction.

The more you know about yourself, the broader is your base, and therefore the higher you can reach. The broader your base, the more self-sufficient you are, and the more you can help others because you are grounded, balanced, rooted. In gung fu (martial arts), balance is all important. If you're not balanced, you cannot effectively defend yourself nor can you engage your aggressor. In gung fu, you must first achieve and maintain physical balance, be rooted and grounded to be effective.

As you attempt to reach up to another level, to improve your circumstances either personally or professionally, you will need a solid base. I refer to this as building a platform. Think of a solid platform that you are trying to build, with solid concrete footings and massive structure to support you on your ascent to the next level. Being balanced is part of this platform. The platform you will build will be level, adapting to the landscape underneath, but solid and firm. You can build such a professional platform, step up on it and use it to reach the next level in your career—but only if your platform is balanced.

175

Balance is what this chapter is all about—achieving balance in your daily life, so you are grounded and rooted, able to care for all your personal, professional, physical, and even spiritual needs. You will then have sufficient and (even) surplus resources to help others—your spouse, children, parents, place of worship, community—nation. But it begins with you, with you standing on a balanced platform.

How will you know if you are in balance? Introspection is the tool to determine this. Self analysis—not self-criticism—is the route. Introspection is simply the act of self-observation. It is as if you stand outside of yourself, taking note of and reporting your conscious inner thoughts, desires, and sensations. We do this in the context of this book to examine and evaluate our own thoughts, feelings, and, in more spiritual cases, even our soul. Basically, it's a contemplation of one's self.

If you accept this advice, about seeking feedback about your attributes and balance, you may not want to start by asking spouses or significant others. Why not ask your spouse? Because they have agendas. They are not bad people, but it's just human nature. We all have agendas when we are discussing the attributes of our spouses, significant others, or partners. It's important to receive honest feedback but without the added baggage and complex dynamics of interpersonal agendas. If a good friend cannot be found for this purpose, then you may have to pay for professional assessment, using a coach, psychologist, social worker, or other credentialed professional. If they are any good, they will hold up a mirror to your personality and make some suggestions about how to achieve balance.

About two years ago I was making a keynote speech at a conference in Portland, Oregon. After my presentation someone in the audience asked, "What if I have trouble with that, with introspection? I don't know how to do that." My response was, "Find a good friend, have a beer with him/her, and ask them some questions about yourself. Tell them that you want some honest feedback about your attributes, and ask them if you are balanced among many priorities. A good friend will tell you the truth."

In another case, I had a client, a young lady with a storied past, who wanted to be introspective but had been judged so harshly by others that all she saw in herself was bad, negative, unworthy. It took several hours of weekly sessions just to get the point across to her that *I accepted her exactly as she was*, and those words, those few words—"I accept you exactly as you are . . ." were words she couldn't assimilate because it was so distant from what she had been experiencing from family. Once she understood that, we were then able to establish this as a firm platform, where she believed in herself sufficiently, enabling us to proceed with her career choices.

Let's take a look at how to achieve balance in the three most important aspects of your life: mind, body, and spirit.

The Mind of a Lifelong Learner

Growth is the only evidence of life.
—John Henry Cardinal Newman

Lifelong learners, no matter how old they are, are curious, have an insatiable appetite for information, and manage to keep up with recent developments in many parts of the world. My mother, Zoila, is an example. She is ninety-three years old as I write this, living alone, and maintaining a three-bedroom house in Miami, Florida. When I call her on the telephone from New York every day, I know that I should have my homework done and have the latest news headlines at hand because she will quiz me about news developments. She will unfailingly call me out if I don't know the latest from every corner of the world—as she does. She reads the *Miami Herald*, in English and in Spanish, so she stays abreast of developments in the western hemisphere and in Europe. Her friends and family come to visit, and she is eager to exchange information and the latest world developments. My mother stays physically very active, looking after her house on a daily basis, cooking for herself and others (she has someone come once a week to look after the yard and a handy lady to help her with major housecleaning chores). The point is that my mother is proud of her age, and by staying physically and mentally active on a daily basis, she has outlived everyone in the extended family.

Another example of a lifelong learner is Fred Gorstein. I met Dr. Fred (as his friends call him) when he brought his late model Porsche 911 to the race track, Pocono International Raceway in Pennsylvania, to learn how to drive his sports car really fast. I was one of the track instructors for Dr. Fred, and in him I now have a wonderful friend. Dr. Fred is very sociable, approachable, humble, and most of all, a sponge for information and facts about everything, especially how to drive faster! But he is a lot more than that. Dr. Fred is actually Fred Gorstein, MD, and the chairman emeritus of the Department of Pathology, Anatomy, and Cell Biology at Thomas Jefferson University Medical Center in Philadelphia. Until recently, Dr. Fred coordinated the work of several hundred medical faculty, technologists, and others who reported to him as they engaged in research, the education of medical students, residents in pathology, and patient care. He still works full-time teaching and performing patient care responsibilities. The university has retained him far beyond the usual retirement age of around sixty or sixty-five.

Let's hear from Dr. Fred directly, as he elaborates on the merits of lifelong learning.

Thoughts of a Lifelong Learner

—Curiosity May Kill Cats, but not Learners. Self directed
Learning (SDL) is the Key

By Dr. Fred Gorstein

I have always been curious about the world around us, and especially the mysteries of our incredible body. This insatiable need to know led me to Brooklyn Technical High School, in New York. There, we conducted experiments, built a house, worked in a forge shop and learned to design tools. We were fortunate that our teachers fostered independent learning.

This system was ahead of its time because our educational approach then and now is prescriptive and fails to stimulate curiosity and the thirst for learning. How do we nurture the innate curiosity of our children and carry it forward to adulthood? Stimulating curiosity is especially important in the education of a physician. No physician can long be effective if not committed to "lifelong learning". Hence, one of the goals of our medical education system is the stimulation of lifelong, self-directed learning, driven by curiosity, and use of evidence-based information in management of their patients.

Recently I met with a group of my medical students for a discussion. They asked for my comments about their progress in our course. I replied, "My major complaint is that too often you (collective you) seem more concerned about passing the tests and your grades, rather than truly understanding the content". Their reply was swift, "Well, Doctor Gorstein, you made us that way. Since kindergarten, our teachers and parents have judged us by our grades and not much else". How can we change this orientation? One example of such efforts includes teaching using self-directed-learning, SDL. With SDL, control gradually shifts from teacher to learner. Learners exercise a great deal of independence—setting learning goals and deciding what is worthwhile learning. Learning how to convey new information to others is the best learning tool.

One approach that we use in medical school is problem-based-learning (PBL). The PBL setting consists of a small group with a single faculty (facilitator), conducted in two phases. In phase 1, a clinical case is presented. Students are asked to define the problem(s) and develop a list of possible differential diagnoses. Students are then expected to indicate what additional information needed to establish or exclude the diagnosis. Students refer to texts or other sources. In preparation for phase 2, students choose a subject related to a possible diagnosis to report on (teach). The facilitator's job is mostly finished at this point, because in phase 2 the students teach the group. In my experience, everyone, including the faculty learns—each student becomes a teacher while learning. Teaching skills are especially important for a physician where communication skills are key to successful physician-patient relationships and peer education. One might note that the Latin root of doctor is "doctour" or "docere" to teach.

In self-directed learning, the most important role of the mentor is to stimulate curiosity and provide some of the tools for inquiry.

Dr. Fred's high-speed track driving skills have been improving steadily, and in 2009, the Philadelphia Region Porsche Club of America honored him as Driver of the Year. Dr. Fred is eighty years old.

On Balance

The emphasis of this chapter is balance. But I'll be the first to admit that at times I have been off-balance. For example, there was a time in my life, when my children were very little, that I was off-balance, pursuing my learning agenda at my family's expense.

Learning takes many forms, and college courses are just one of them. Although I have not taken a formal college course in many years, I have continued to learn via conferences and informal channels about science, technology, history, art, languages, music, politics, geography, cultures, and about people—mostly about people.

In recent years I have seen people react to downward economic impact by joining a college class or going to graduate school. This phenomenon is occurring even as I write this second edition. The economic impact of 2008 and 2009 has left millions unemployed, and many thousands are enrolling in colleges and universities. For example, the Massachusetts Institute of Technology has experienced a 30 percent increase in enrollment applications for their MBA program in the most recent semester, a statistic replicated in other colleges across the nation. Going back to college is a wise investment but a very expensive one, so think before you enroll. There may be alternatives, like certification in your area of expertise. This would be much faster than a master's degree and may be all you need.

Let's take a look at other aspects of life balance.

Break Sweat

You can't just exercise your brain. Your body needs to do something physical. Part of maintaining appropriate balance is physical activity. Do whatever you like: swimming, biking, power walking, weight lifting, gung fu, Pilates, yoga, basketball, etc. The key is *you have to break sweat*. Breaking sweat releases endorphins, which will elevate your mood and your spirits. The more "down" you feel, the more you need to get a good workout.

I've discovered a whole new world at the gym. About ten years ago I joined the YMCA (Southeast Branch, Pittsford, New York) and over time have made many friends there. This is a beneficial byproduct of joining a health club—you not only reap the benefits of physical activity, but if you take off your iPod earphones and smile, you'll meet many, many wonderful people with similar interests in physical fitness. Need I mention that this also presents excellent networking opportunities?

Let's hear about balance and the need for physical activity from Ron Gordon, a certified personal trainer:

The Mind Body Connection
By Ron Gordon—Personal Trainer to Executives

It is very easy in our hectic business world to put aside our basic need for physical activity and movement. Other things seem more important and certainly more comfortable most of our waking day. However, our need for activity is fundamental to our existence. We are designed to move and be active. As a leader you must invest the time to do the things that are most important to your success. A sedentary lifestyle is problematic and actually ages and stresses our bodies. An active lifestyle pays great personal and business returns.

The good news is that we can take advantage of science and get optimal results in return for a short time investment in exercising.

Of course it is imperative to get your doctor's approval before starting any exercise program, and you will find nothing but encouragement from your doctor. Additionally, if you have never exercised before you need to start slowly and build your body up to its natural capacity.

One of the best ROIs you will find is the dividend you get when you work out hard enough to break a sweat. It doesn't have to be for long, but you need to sweat during your workout three or four times a week, minimally. Working out hard enough to break a sweat will cause many positive things to happen to your body including the release of endorphins. The endorphins have many positive effects, once released, including helping you to relax. Sometimes this relaxing effect is known as a runner's high, but you don't have to run long distances to experience these benefits.

The endorphin release will improve your quality of life immediately. You will notice an increased energy, alertness, and a new ability to focus. Problems that you were struggling with before will seem easier with your new perspective.

First scientifically proven in a 1987 New England Journal of Medicine study, your fitness routine will also add to the longevity of your life. The proven return is that for every hour you exercise vigorously, you will get that back plus two more hours added to your life. You will literally live longer because you workout.

A good exercise program will also make your life easier. All activities and human movements come down to stepping, squatting, pushing, pulling, extending and rotating. The more you practice these activities in a purposeful way, the more efficient you perform all daily routine activities, for instance, going to the store.

The best workout is the one that you will do with consistency over a long period of time. Look for workouts that are fun and involve a variety of exercises. We are all different in that regard, but running, martial arts, yoga, cycling, sailing, skiing, tennis, strength training, dancing, walking, rowing, and exercise class are great examples.

Routinely devote time to break a sweat, three of four times a week, with a good exercise routine and you will feel better, look better, have more energy, be more productive, and live longer.

You can contact Ron Gordon at: rgordonjr@msn.com

Going to the gymnasium or exercise club and sitting at a stationary bicycle, reading a book, listening to music via your iPod earphones on without a trickle of sweat running down your temple is a complete waste of your time.

There is no substitute for breaking sweat.
And you have dozens of choices on how to do it. Your spouse, significant other, and other loved ones will appreciate it. So will your heart.

An Inspirational Story

To get anything worth having, it's a struggle.
—Pamela Iuppa

Pam is a personal trainer. I have many friends who are trainers, but I chose to interview Pamela because she is different. Pam is alive today thanks to a donated kidney, but there is a lot more to her story. Pam works a daunting schedule, with as much as forty-five billable training hours over several gyms every week! She is very successful in her business, but it wasn't easy for Pam to get to this point. Her story should inspire those who have significant obstacles or disabilities. Although I've known her for about ten years, I asked her some questions to obtain her perspective.

"You never know when it's going to end, so take it when you can get it," she said. Pam is always looking for opportunities to train clients, which she obtains by word-of-mouth referrals. She knows that a personal trainer is a discretionary expense, which can be easily ended, so Pam is always considering new clients. Few people can keep up with Pam's seven-day-a-week work schedule. But how did she get started?

Twenty-five years ago, Pam was "wallowing in self-pity." She had been working in an insurance company but felt weak and tired constantly. Her illness was diagnosed as IgA nephropathy, a condition where her kidneys were found to be quickly deteriorating. Medical therapy arrested the condition, but she had already lost 72 percent of her kidney function. She was told that within five years she would be on dialysis and should not attempt to have children. As a young woman, this was very disconcerting to her.

"For six months I felt sorry for myself. I couldn't have my own kids, was told I couldn't have a normal life. But I got tired of feeling weak and helpless, so I started my own training, walking, just walking with one of the trainers at the [Pittsford YMCA]. Later on I began swimming, biking, and I did that for 5 years before I could start training with weights. I saw the improvements. My doctor saw how much I was doing so he encouraged me to do weight training to help avoid osteoporosis. The doctor also signed off that I could adopt a child, my daughter. Then after adopting, I got pregnant and had a boy [he is in college today]."

Over time, Pam has overcome this major kidney dysfunction obstacle, with frequent visits to laboratories for blood work to identify progress/setbacks in her kidney function. She waited patiently for years for a kidney, getting many false starts for a perfect match, and finally received one on in 2009.

To encourage her clients, she advises them, "The physical is far more about your mental state. It's doing what you can, knowing what you can do, and then just doing it!"

Pam sees many who say, "I can't do this, I can't do that." But she says they haven't even tried. And they don't even have the obstacles that Pam had, with only 28 percent kidney function, which inhibits getting rid of toxins normally generated during exercise.

As a personal trainer, Pam has a vision for her enterprise: "To make people see that they are strong, no matter what their disability or inability, to help them see what they can do, not what they can't."

Pam chose to become self-employed over the years and now would not go back to being on someone's payroll.

"I feel I will always be employed, if I want to be, as a trainer."

When asked if she created a plan for her business, Pam said, "No, I just put one foot in front of the other, and people came and started asking for me. I saw other trainers who were successful, and I also consult with physical and occupational therapists, on my own time, I meet them and learn about their methods. I also go in to see them with my clients so they can continue to improve with my training. Some PTs are actually my clients, and they borrow some of my ideas for their practice."

She said some clients come in and they want instant results—they want it yesterday! She uses a metaphor, climbing a long hill on her bike, to illustrate: "Early on in my training, there was this hill that I wanted to climb on my bike, but I couldn't get to the top. After trying over many times, I started just looking down at each rock that I passed by, each rock was a milestone that I had accomplished, and then I got to the top. Training may not show obvious effects for a few weeks, but the improvements will be there. You just have to be willing to work the process."

As a lifelong learner, Pam never ceases to look for fresh ideas. She advises, "Don't be afraid to start at the bottom, and never stop learning. I still go to bed reading books about training. You can't stop learning. You can't afford to get comfortable."

The Spirit: On the Importance of Quiet Introspection

At the risk of sounding removed from reality, I have found from experience that it's important to sit quietly and just listen. Listen to what? To your intuition, your instincts, your contemplative thoughts and insights—to God's will for you. Now, wait, gentle reader, don't leave me yet. I only ask that you try it. There are many ways to do this. You can develop your own. This is the way I do it.

Every morning I wake up very early. I go to the kitchen and make myself a double espresso. I take my espresso to the garden room, sit in a particular chair facing a window in the east, and watch the sun rise (weather and season permitting). During this very quiet time I don't let other noises interrupt. I can see the sun rise for about nine months a year, in this part of upstate New York. In other months, I look out through the window, yes, in the dark, at the lights from a hilltop hotel about two miles away. What's all this have to do with strategies and tactics for career decisions? The point being made is that you should make time for quiet introspection, renewal, reenergizing.

This quiet introspection is different than prayer. I often finish my quiet interludes with prayer. In prayer we are often asking for or giving thanks for something. In a quiet interlude, however, the emphasis, the objective is to quiet our minds and spirits—and just listen.

Try it!

You won't even need the espresso.

Here's another view of the spiritual context by Korey Finstad, a Lutheran minister:

Discerning our Spiritual Calling
By Korey Finstad

Our careers often say a lot about who we are. Our profession makes up a large part of our identity. For people of faith seeking to be disciples of Christ, it only makes sense that we try to choose our career as an extension of our identity as a disciple. Some choose to join the clergy, but society needs various roles to be filled to function. Each of these roles is as important as another. What a mess we would be in if everyone left their various occupations to become a priest, pastor, rabbi or imam! You can serve your neighbor by running a business to provide needed goods, building a road, or coaching his children.

The question becomes which career is right for you to fulfill your calling to be a disciple. We would love to hear a voice from a burning bush telling us clearly what we should do, but it is rarely that easy. The truth is that we may try many times to find that right niche, and that even the right niche may change with time. Perhaps we go through many learning and growing experiences before truly being ready for that perfect role for us.

Whatever that niche may be, not only will it be fulfilling a need for society, it will be something we're good at. Each of us has unique skills and talents given to us by God, and we feel good about ourselves when we do them. Doesn't it make sense that the role in society that God would want us to do would fit well with the talents that God has given us?

Not only would we be good at our niche, we would enjoy doing it. I am often awestruck as I observe people enjoying jobs that I would hate doing. It just goes to show that people are created differently and have different things that they like to do. What a wise God we have to create us so! I suspect that some people are sitting waiting for God to show them what to do, when God is waiting for them to determine what it is that they want to do.

Whether we have found our niche yet or not, it is important to remember we serve God by serving our neighbors. We should be in constant conversation with God to discern the best way for us to do that. We faithfully trust that God lovingly leads us towards a life that is filled with joy and fulfillment.

Korey Finstad
koreyfinstad@msn.com

The Seven-Dollar Sneakers

What drives you? What keeps you going? What do you visualize as success? As a reason for driving your very best—to finish the race? To win?

I was born and raised in Cuba. As I was growing up, there was a great revolution. Thousands joined Fidel Castro in the mountains. In fact, my aunt and uncle joined Castro's revolution—they were guerrilla fighters in Castro's army. Then in 1959, Castro's army won the war. We thought we had a great future!

But in just one year, Castro took over all businesses, gagged all the media, and began separating children from families. I was only eleven, and the government had me marching in parades with my little army uniform.

My parents said, "Enough!" They decided that I would not be conscripted. My parents then sent me to the United States.

I arrived in Miami, and months later, my parents decided to leave Cuba. They were in their forties at that time, and they knew that they would have to leave everything behind. My parents took my baby sister, and they left everything right where it was—the house, the furniture, refrigerator, TV, Hi-Fi—the Mercury on the driveway—absolutely everything. In Cuba you had to behave on a daily basis as if everything is perfectly normal. Then one day you call a taxi, you go the airport, and you never come back.

So I was already here, in Miami, when my parents arrived in the United States. After they arrived, my dad—I called him Papi—had to find work. He had been an accountant in Havana, but he didn't speak English.

Papi's first job in Miami was working as an auto mechanic, but he was exploited and paid only $40 in cash after working sixty hours. Papi then said, "We have to leave Miami." The government gave us a one-way ticket to Philadelphia. It was winter, and we went to Penn's Grove, a tiny town in New Jersey. All we had was our summer clothes from Cuba.

Papi landed a job as a janitor in a diner. He was bringing home $42.08 a week. Mami and Papi stretched those forty-two bucks—paying rent, utilities, and buying food for four. Christmas came and went that year, but they couldn't buy anything.

Papi learned some English and was promoted to office clerk. I remember when he announced this promotion. I said to Mami, "Now we don't have to cut the paper napkins in half!" Every week my parents used to put all the cash money on the bed, spread it around, and say, "This is for the rent, this for the food, and this for the electric . . ." That's how I learned about budgeting.

Then Papi got laid off, but a few months later he landed an accounting job in Dover, Delaware. This was a gift from God, a good job with benefits! But we had to move from New Jersey to Delaware.

Because of all the moving around, I had attended five schools in three years. I was a freshman in Dover High School. I told Papi that I wanted to play basketball, but I needed sneakers. All I had was a pair of leather shoes.

My parents agreed that I should play, so we went shopping for sneakers. I knew at that time that we were poor, that going out to purchase a pair of shoes was outside our budget.

We found a pair of black high-top sneakers for seven bucks. Seven dollars was significant hit to our fragile weekly budget. Papi figured out a way, and he paid for the shoes.

I was so excited with my new seven-dollar sneakers! I even kept the box they came in. I kept the boxes of things I got because it was so rare to be able to get something that even the box had value. The next day after school, I had my new seven-dollar sneakers, and I was ready to play! But these were tryouts. I had to prove to the coach that I could make the junior varsity team. This was another cultural adjustment for me. At the gym, they made all the boys go through some basketball drills. Then they blindfolded all the kids and asked us to dribble the basketball. Well, dribbling while blindfolded was not a skill I had perfected, so after kicking the basketball around the gym a few times, I was quickly dismissed.

Waiting for Papi to pick me up, I thought about what I would say. Here I was, with my brand-new seven-dollar sneakers, but I didn't make the team. I remember thinking, *Papi is out seven bucks and I am done with basketball. How can I make it up to Papi?*

When Papi picked me up in his old '55 Chevy, I sat in the front seat. He asked me, "How did it go?" Then I explained what happened, that I was dismissed because I wasn't good enough. He said, "That's not right!" But I explained, "Well, I know, Papi, but that's how it's done."

To this day, as I tell you, it still hits me. It hits me hard.

So I ask you now, What drives you? What keeps you going? What do you visualize as success? As a reason for driving your very best—to finish the race? To win?

What drives me? What drives me is making it up to Papi.

Love all.
Trust a few.
Hurt none.
—William Shakespeare

ATTACHMENT A

LOVE TO DO

SKILLS

ATTRIBUTES

ATTACHMENT B

EXAMPLES OF ELEVATOR SPEECHES

- *Business growth executive excelling at strategy and leadership. Extensive experience working at the intersection of marketing, product development, and customer engagement. Proven success in market introduction of new technology products and services. Accomplished in integrated product and services marketing. Highly ethical, creative, results focused leader who thrives in challenging environments and builds enduring, trusted relationships.*

- *Results-oriented leader with proven success analyzing markets and businesses, identifying market opportunities, and developing strategies to leverage competitive advantage. Adept in developing innovative solutions to multidimensional problems. Uncommon ability to learn quickly to rapidly distill complex business problems to their core issues. Very curious and critical thinker who can apply extensive experience from a variety of industries to drive revenue growth and profitability. Effective speaker to C-level audiences, directors, and large groups.*

(This management consultant for the renewable resources industry said that he had sent out "zillions" of cover letters and resumes, with no results. He has a PhD in engineering plus an MBA. We met for CC-101, discussed how to present his attributes in his cover letter and resume. He sent one new cover letter and resume, emphasizing his attributes—not just his skills and experience—and the targeted company called him three times the following day. He and his wife were incredulous.)

- *Enterprising and articulate business professional with the proven ability to manage multiple tasks and accomplish objectives in a fast-paced environment. Customer-oriented individual with outstanding communication, organizational, and interpersonal skills demonstrated by the ability to work with people of diverse backgrounds. Experience with providing written and oral business presentations.*

(This is the elevator speech of Donna Highsmith, thirty-two years old, who landed a well-paid position as internal communications director for a national security company in Florida's Gold Coast.)

- *Accomplished accounting and finance professional with an extensive background in accounting, financial planning, internal and external reporting, Sarbanes-Oxley/IFRS compliance, SAP implementation, process improvement, and project management with large domestic and international companies. Proficient in SEC reporting. Managed and prepared 10-Ks, 10-Qs, related disclosure checklist and earnings release for a $16 billion global company. Prepared and analyzed the cash flow statement, headcount, shares outstanding, lease footnote, and capitalized interest footnote for the 10-K.*

(Sharp, elegant, impressive financial executive in Fortune 50 company, with extensive consulting experience)

- *Results-driven, enthusiastic, tenacious office management professional desiring opportunity to utilize my skills, experience, and attributes to generate revenue and maintain customer relationships, contract administration, and process optimization for professional services organization.*

(With only a high school education, Tara accepted a supervisor's position at a blue chip company paying $55,000.)

- *Articulate, well-organized consulting professional with business-to-business experience and particular skills in relationship building, business and project analysis, and customer management. Excellent track record with sales performance, consultation, and achieving market penetration.*

- *Mature, punctual college student seeking summer full-time and school year part-time employment to defray college expenses. Detail oriented, mechanically inclined with strong customer service skills. Demonstrates exceptional problem-solving abilities, enjoys working in teams, and is very logical.*

(This twenty-year-old high school graduate landed an entry-level technical position with a nationally renowned Porsche racing engine rebuilding business.)

- *Creative, dedicated, and passionate music educator, offering effective communications with exceptional musicianship, teaching, and presentation skills; high degree of professionalism, decision making, and problem solving; superior project design and program management; supervisory experience; appreciation for aesthetics, eye and ear for detail; versatility and human compassion.*

(This music educator was not receiving any responses to her resumes until she included language about her attributes in her elevator speech and in her cover letter.)

- *Resourceful, enthusiastic, and entrepreneurial human resources leader with demonstrable accomplishments as strategic partner to senior leaders of manufacturing, health care, academic, business services, multiunion and multinational enterprises. Seeking opportunity in organization needing seasoned trusted advisor and operational leader for growth.*

(Successful human resources consultant.)

- *Assertive problem solver with excellent leadership and strategic business development skills. Reliable and adaptive team player who is passionate about applying diverse industry experience to drive incremental revenue growth and inspire customers. Recognized as an exemplary contributor with an ability to exceed expectations and foster long-term partnerships with team members, vendors, and customers.*

(This gentleman is one of the most successful sales engineers I've ever known.)

- *Effective leader in development strategies that support business growth. Accomplished training and development program manager and facilitator with experience in development, deployment, and administration of training solutions that get results. Recognized as exceptional organizer with strong project and people management skills. Engaging interpersonal style, process oriented, and effective at building coalitions. Consistent record as a customer satisfaction enabler with business maturity and a solid work ethic.*

(Very successful international training professional wielding "big company" ideas with small group delivery.)

- *Experienced leader with extensive environmental, health, and safety (EHS) expertise in developing and implementing global programs. Creatively solve problems and drive solutions with a unique ability to leverage business acumen and technical knowledge. Management Black Belt adept at using lean principles to optimize work processes, improve efficiency, and reduce costs. Fluent in Spanish.*

(Highly successful EHS professional with global responsibility in Fortune 100 company)

- *Dynamic, results-oriented leader with proven success in analyzing customer and business needs and developing strategies that support high-growth environments. Customer oriented, with outstanding communications and interpersonal skills. Recognized ability to work across boundaries and motivate teams to drive innovative solutions to multidimensional problems. Resourceful, critical thinker who can apply extensive experience from a variety of disciplines to derive operational excellence worldwide.*

(Seasoned Fortune 500 quality, service, and support manager)

ATTACHMENT C

COVER LETTER TEMPLATE

Your Name
Your Address
City, State Zip

Telephone   **Email address**

Prospect Name
Prospect Title
Address
City, State, Zip

Today's Date

Dear ＿＿＿＿＿＿＿,

    I was referred to you by [name]. My purpose in writing is to explore how my skills [name some], experience [name some], and personal attributes [name two] may be of value to [company name].

    Your organization is of great interest to me because I have been [briefly explain relevant skills and experience to the target opportunity]. As you can see in my resume (enclosed) in my work I love to [briefly describe those things that you love to do in your current or past employment]. My customers [or clients or peers or managers] say that I have a passion for, and that they can see that I love to ＿＿＿＿＿＿＿.

    Perhaps your organization can take advantage of my [attribute], [attribute], and [attribute] to [improve sales/improve customer satisfaction/reduce cost/improve margins]. I will be calling your office on [date and time] to follow up.

Sincerely,
Your Name
/enc.

ATTACHMENT D

JUNE FARNSWORTH
1520 Ethereal Crescent
Farnorth, New York, 17869

Home 598/987-6842
Cell 598/869-7480
myhouse@yahoo.rr.com

CAREER SUMMARY

Effective **leader in development strategies that support business growth**. Accomplished training and development program manager and facilitator with experience in the development, deployment, and administration of training solutions that get results. Recognized as an exceptional organizer with strong project and people management skills. Engaging interpersonal style, process oriented, and effective at building coalitions. Consistent record as a customer satisfaction enabler with business maturity and a solid work ethic.

PROFESSIONAL EXPERIENCE
FAROUT CORPORATION, Farnorth, New York, 1984-2006

Development Manager, Developing Operations 2004-2006

Managed the development function for an organization of 9,000 direct and indirect employees across forty-four countries in Latin America and Eastern Europe. Built a direct team of US-based development program managers and a global network of regional training and development managers. Improved the capability of overseas sales populations through the deployment of effective and efficient development principles, practices, and tools. Created development standards, expectations, and measurements that built employee competencies and an environment of continuous learning. Provided courses and learning materials that enabled effective field deployment to bridge the skills and performance gaps toward advancing our business objectives.

- Created standardized job profiles and learning paths for field sales, sales management, and technical roles.
- Established a global development network for consistent deployment of training programs, across geographies with varying levels of training support, delivery capability, and learning practices.
- Implemented a sales management process and training program, which improved consistency of sales tracking and support processes.
- Created annual training plan delivery metrics and process, which enabled the support and inspection of training delivery required to build needed skills and competencies.
- Facilitated steps toward a global management and leadership development by coordinating sharing among various FAROUT development groups that create similar programs for their specific geographies.
- Respected participant on the human resources leadership team.

Manager, Launch, Learning, and Communications for field technical sales population 2000-2003

Managed team of six launch managers who rolled out new products and solutions to field populations. Developed and communicated product support strategies to technical sales support populations.

- Designed and implemented processes to ensure technical sales force had reliable methods to obtain the technical and marketing information they needed to support the sales cycle. Provided field-training strategy/direction.
- Expedited field sales support training by collecting requirements and engaging the education organization to create alternative solutions that could be delivered earlier than standard programs, addressing significant knowledge gaps caused by staff reductions.

Manager, Technical Operations Programs and Strategies 1998-2000

Managed a team of five direct reports who created and implemented product launch programs for a newly formed technical field organization.

- Redesigned field customer trainer job structure to reflect increase in technical skill levels required to support networked products. Assessed and reassigned each trainer against these new job requirements to ensure that their title and grade accurately reflected their current experience and skill level.

Manager, Customer Education Marketing and Development Programs 1996-1998

Managed six direct reports who created marketing collaterals, customer training materials and implemented marketing programs for field and training organizations.

- Reduced training materials development costs by 10 percent.
- Reversed wave of customer dissatisfaction by standardizing product training outputs and materials across all product development teams and in ten different countries.

Manager, Customer Education National Reprographic Program 1994-1995

Managed four direct reports who designed and rolled out new fee-based training program for reprographic products.

- Defined field training job responsibilities, grade levels, compensation structure, and training plans.
- Created and tracked revenue plans for this new line of business and created manpower and contracting plans.
- Enhanced the ability to attract higher skilled trainers by convincing senior management of the need to convert nonexempt field trainer jobs to exempt levels. This was critical to justify the new practice of charging customers for training that had previously been provided free of charge.

Manager, Customer Education Marketing 1993

Managed ten direct reports who developed marketing collaterals that were used by external and internal customers to understand the choices and benefits of training offerings. Represented the San Francisco-based customer education organization in Farnorth headquarters and acted as liaison for all functions.

Manager, Customer Education Training Development, Los Angeles, California 1988-1992

Managed a team of fifteen training developers who created customer training instructor guides and student workbooks used to deliver fee-based customer training on systems products. Supplied all Farout operating divisions with documentation and training materials for output, internal, and outsourced product manufacturing.

Training Analyst, San Diego, California 1983-1987

Wrote printing systems operator guides and training materials used by field analysts to train customers. Delivered train-the-trainer sessions to new-hire analyst classes.

PRIOR EXPERIENCE

LAIDBACK CENTER and LIFESTYLES, INC., Sausalito, California 1977-1982

Hired, trained, and managed sales and delivery staff of fifteen for a retail furniture store. Sold furniture and provided decorating services to customers who purchased substantial orders.

ADVANCED DEVELOPMENT CENTER, Laguna Beach, California 1974-1976

Developed individualized lesson plans and taught students who were experiencing self-concept challenges in Southern Beach School District kindergarten or private preschool programs.

EDUCATION AND COMPUTER SKILLS
BA Psychology, Domain University, California, 1977
Microsoft Office Suite: Word, PowerPoint, Excel

PROFESSIONAL ASSOCIATION
National and local Member of America Society of Training and
Development (ASTD)
Vice President of Professional Development Programs for Farnorth ASTD

Attachment E

THE T-CHART FOR INTERVIEWING

What do they want/need?	What can I offer/contribute?

Attachment F

COLD NETWORKING CALL

- Hello, my name is _____.
- *[Name]* suggested I give you a call. S/he felt that you would be a good person to offer me some tips or advice.
- I know you are very busy, so I won't take up too much of your time.
- I am in a career transition at this time, and I am interested in how businesses that you know handle their *[problems with which you have skills and expertise]*.
- May I set up a short meeting with you, at your convenience, to obtain your feedback about the types of industries and companies that I am targeting in my search?
- *[Name]* thought you could be very helpful to me in this way.
- You can call me at my number, *[your number]*. I will also send you an e-mail with my contact information, in case that works better for you.
- Thank you, and I look forward to meeting with you.

Attachment G

WARM NETWORKING CALL

- Hello, this is *[your name]*. You may recall, we know each other from *[mention how you met]*.
- I know you are very busy, so I won't take up too much of your time, but I was thinking that you would be a good person to offer me some suggestions.
- Currently I am in career transition, and I am interested in how other organizations in the area manage their *[problems about which you, the reader, have skills and experience]*.
- With your permission I would like to set up a short meeting with you, at your convenience, to obtain your perspectives and insights about the industries that I am targeting.
- If you'd like, you can call me at my number, *[your number]*. I will also send you an e-mail with my contact information, in case that works better for you.
- Thank you and I look forward to meeting with you!

APPENDIX

Attributes	
Academic	Intelligent
Accurate	Introspective
Active	Intuitive
Action oriented	It's a jungle out there
Accurate, detailed	Investigative/measured
Adaptable	Kind
Adventurous	Leader
Aggressive	Low profile
Ambitious	Loyal
Analytical	Mellow, quiet
Artistic	Motivated
Assertive	Needs prodding, deadlines
Authoritative	Open minded
Balanced	Optimistic
Broad minded	Orderly
Calm under pressure	Organized
Candid	Outgoing
Capable	Passionate

Careful	Passive
Caring	Patient
Cautious	Perceptive
Charismatic	Persevering
Clever	Personable
Communicative	Persuasive
Compassionate	Poised
Competent	Polite
Competitive	Politically savvy
Confident	Positive
Conscientious	Practical
Conservative	Precise
Considerate	Prefer structure, process
Cooperative	Problem solver
Contemplative	Progressive
Cost conscious	Prudent
Creative	Punctual
Dependable	Quick study
Dependent on structure	Rational
Determined	Realistic
Diplomatic	Reasonable
Direct	Reflective
Disciplined	Relaxed
Discreet	Reliable
Eager	Reserved
Easygoing	Resourceful
Effective	Responsible
Efficient	Responsive/Quick
Energetic	Results oriented

Enthusiastic	Risk adverse
Entrepreneurial	Risk taker
Ethical	Safety conscious
Expressive	Satisfied
Fair minded	Self-controlled / managed
Fast learner	Self-starter
Firm	Sensible
Flexible	Serious
Focused	Shrewd
Follower	Sincere
Frugal	Shy
Fun	Sociable
Generous	Solo practitioner
Gentle	Spontaneous
Goal oriented	Stable
Hard worker	Steady
Helpful	Strategic
High standards	Strong
High tolerance for ambiguity	Successful
Highly energized	Sympathetic
Honest	Tactful
Humorous	Team player
Idealistic	Thorough
Imaginative	Visionary
Independent	Warm
Innovative	Withdrawn / introverted
Inscrutable	Witty

Suggested Reading

Mitch Albom, *Tuesdays with Morrie: An Old Man, a Young Man, and Life's Greatest Lesson* (Broadway Books, 1997).

Arnold Boldt, *Resumes for the Rest of Us: Secrets from the Pros for Job Seekers with Unconventional Career Paths* (Career Press, 2008).

Richard Bolles, *What Color Is Your Parachute? A Practical Guide for Job-Hunters and Career Changers* (Berkeley: Ten Speed Press, 2006).

Timothy Butler, *Getting Unstuck: How Dead Ends Become New Paths* (Boston: Harvard Business School Press, 2007).

Keith Ferrazzi, with Tahl Raz: *Never Eat Alone and Other Secrets to Success, One Relationship at a Time* (New York: Currency-Doubleday, 2005).

Napoleon Hill, *Think and Grow Rich* (Ballantine Books, 1960)

W. Chan Kim and Reneé Mauborgne, *Blue Ocean Strategy: How to Create Uncontested Market Space and Make the Competition Irrelevant* (Harvard Business School Press, 2005).

Dan Miller, *48 Days to the Work You Love* (Tennessee: B&H Publishing Group, 2007).

Orville Pierson, *The Unwritten Rules of the Highly Effective Job Search: The Proven Program Used by the World's Leading Career Services Company* (New York: McGraw Hill, 2006).

Susan Scott, *Fierce Conversations: Achieving Success at Work & in Life, One Conversation at a Time* (New York: Viking, 2002).

Paul Tieger and Barbara Barron, *Do What You Are: Discover the Perfect Career for You Through the Secrets of Personality Type* (3rd ed. 2001).

Michael Watkins, *The First 90 Days: Critical Success Strategies for New Leaders at All Levels* (Boston: Harvard Business School Publishing, 2003).

Margaret J. Wheatley, *Leadership and the New Science: Learning About Organization from an Orderly Universe* (San Francisco: Berrett-Koehler Publishers, Inc., 1994).

Notes and References

(NB: It is with utmost sadness that I report that while I was drafting this book, I discovered that George Longshore was killed in Washington DC. George was taken from us way too soon. My sincerest condolences to his wife and family)

Alan Breznick, *Mastering the Art of Selection* (Cornell Enterprise, fall 2004).

Perri Capell, *The Right Time to Talk About Salary* (The Wall Street Journal Online, January 23, 2007).

Cornell Career Services. *Career Guide 2005/2006* (Ithaca, NY: Cornell Career Services, Cornell University).

Carlos Eire, *Waiting for Snow in Havana: Confessions of a Cuban Boy* (The Free Press, 2003).

Tom Ferguson, MD, *e-Patients: How They Can Help Us Heal Healthcare*, Supported by the Robert Wood Johnson Foundation Quality Health Care Grant #043806, 2007.

Cheryl Gilman, *Doing Work You Love: Discovering Your Purpose and Realizing Your Dreams* (Barnes & Noble/McGraw Hill, 1997).

John Grohol, PhD, *International Society of Mental Health Online*, http://www.ismho.org/home.asp.

Fali Huang and Peter Cappelli. *Employee Screening: Theory and Evidence*. http://papers.nber.org/papers/w12071.pdf (accessed March 2006).

Steve Jobs, *Commencement Address* (Stanford, CA: Stanford University, June 16, 2005).

Spencer Johnson, *Who Moved My Cheese? An Amazing Way to Deal with Change in Your Work and in Your Life* (New York: G. P. Putnam's Sons, 1998).

Kelly K Spors, "So You Want to Be an Entrepreneur," The Wall Street Journal, February 23, 2009.

Orville Pierson, *The Unwritten Rules of Highly Effective Job Search*. (McGraw Hill, 2006).

Rosa Smith-Montanaro, *Mind Over Platter—Train Your Brain To Think Thin!* (Rochester, NY: 2006).

Kevin Wheeler, *A Letter to Hiring Managers: How to Make Sure You Hire the Best—Five Tips for You as You Work with Your Recruiters* (ERE Daily, September 8, 2006).

"What are the top three rules for jobseekers to follow to successfully negotiate the best possible compensation package?" *http://womenforhire.com.*

Michael D. Zinn, *Executive Search Newsletter,* Volume XVII, Edition I, (Lawrenceville, NJ February 2006).

INDEX